HIKING
LAS VEGAS

HIKING
LAS VEGAS

60 HIKES WITHIN
60 MINUTES OF THE STRIP

Branch Whitney

HUNTINGTON PRESS
Las Vegas, Nevada

Hiking Las Vegas — 60 Hikes Within 60 Minutes of the Strip

Published by
> Huntington Press
> 3687 South Procyon Avenue
> Las Vegas, Nevada 89103
> (702) 252-0655 Phone
> (702) 252-0675 Fax
> e-mail: books@huntingtonpress.com

ISBN 0-929712-21-8

Cover and background photos: Jason Cox
Back cover photos: Branch Whitney & Jeff Scheid
Cover design: Maile Austraw
All interior photos: Branch Whitney
Production: Jason Cox
Interior design: Bethany Coffey & Jason Cox

Printing History
1st Edition — August 1997
Reprinted — April 1998, April 2001

This book is dedicated to Brittney

ACKNOWLEDGMENTS

I would like to thank the following people for their guidance and knowledge: Gene Arnesen, Richard Baugh, Howard Booth, John Carpenter, Frank Davenport, Brett Dawson, Dennis Hayes, Dave Hardy, Greg Sanantos, Lee Schultz, Neil Soberson, and Glenn Stoll.

Extra special thanks to the two best partners anyone could hike with: Eva "Piece of Cake" Pollan and Susan "You're the Best" Murphy.

And to the gang at Huntington Press: Bethany, Jason, Anthony, Len, and especially Deke. It's nice to work with a "real" publishing company.

TABLE OF CONTENTS

GLOSSARY ♦ 269

♦INTRODUCTION♦

Las Vegas is the new vacation capital of the United States, with more than 30 million people visiting every year. If you're looking for something other than gambling at smoky casino tables, or for a vacation that leaves your body in better shape than your wallet, there's good news. Some of the best hiking, rock-scrambling, and bouldering trails in the country are located less than 30 minutes from the Las Vegas Strip. This mecca of hiking is called Red Rock Canyon.

And if you really want to get high while hiking, Mt. Charleston (elevation 11,918) is less than one hour from the Strip. Hikes ranging from 30 minutes to all day long are waiting for anyone who wants clean air, spectacular views, and the serenity of the mountains. For the hiker or rock scrambler, Las Vegas really does have it all. It would be difficult to find another city with this many hiking and scrambling trails within such a short distance.

Hiking Las Vegas covers 60 hikes in Red Rock Canyon and the Mt. Charleston Area. None of the hikes require technical climbing abilities; however, some of the hikes include class II and III sections (explained on p. 9). If you haven't hiked before or you're not in shape, don't attempt the tougher hikes. Start with the easy ones and progress to the more difficult. People who are in good shape will find many of the harder hikes challenging and enjoyable. But no matter what kind of shape you're in, hiking is a great activity that relieves stress and improves cardiovascular fitness, not to mention being one of the best ways to enjoy nature. *Hiking Las Vegas* takes you beyond the lights, congestion, and confusion of Las Vegas to a place where clean air, open space, and magnificent sights await you.

THE PURPOSE OF THIS BOOK

The goal of *Hiking Las Vegas* is to help you enjoy the hikes in Red Rock Canyon and the Mt. Charleston Area. I've rated the hikes according to three different criteria: distance, difficulty, and how easy it is to follow the trail. I've provided explicit directions to the trailheads, photographs of the routes, and trail maps. I've covered all 60 hikes from start (getting to the trailhead) to finish (getting back to the trailhead safely). This is critical when it comes to the hikes at Red Rock, which differs from other hiking and climbing areas. Some of the scrambling routes are so remote that it could be days before another person would come across a lost or stranded hiker. The only way to accurately describe a route is to furnish explicit details coupled with photos, which is what you'll find in the hike descriptions. It would be hard to get lost on the hikes that follow established trails, so the descriptions of these hikes are less detailed.

HOW THIS BOOK IS ORGANIZED

Hiking Las Vegas is divided into two geographical areas: Mt. Charleston and Red Rock Canyon. Directions on how to get to both are provided below. It's important to clear up some confusion about the two; hiking parties often have difficulty linking up due to misunderstandings. We want to spend our time hiking, not waiting at a wrong location.

Mt. Charleston Area
You may have heard of Toiyabe National Forest, the Spring Mountains, Mt. Charleston, Kyle Canyon, Lee Canyon, and

other names of hiking areas near Las Vegas—it can get complicated. Toiyabe National Forest, the largest national forest in the continental United States, covers 3,855,960 acres. It spans an area from eastern California to southern Nevada. Within the Toiyabe lies Spring Mountains National Recreation Area (SMNRA). The 316,000 acres that comprise the SMNRA are managed by the U.S. Forest Service. The SMNRA contains the Mt. Charleston Wilderness Area. Kyle Canyon, Lee Canyon, Mt. Charleston, and Bonanza Mountain are part of the Mt. Charleston Wilderness Area. For simplicity, the Mt. Charleston Wilderness Area will be referred to as "Mt. Charleston" and "the Mt. Charleston Area" in this book.

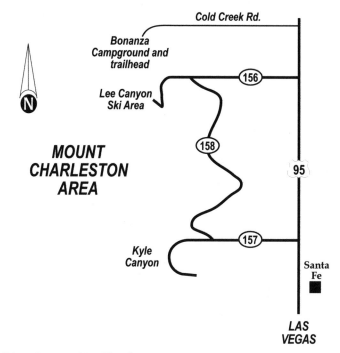

Directions to Mt. Charleston

Mt. Charleston is easy to find. There are two main hiking areas in Mt. Charleston: Kyle Canyon and Lee Canyon. If the trailhead is in Kyle Canyon, take U.S. Highway 95 north to

State Route 157. Turn left (west) onto 157 and travel 17 to 21 miles into Kyle Canyon. When coming from Las Vegas, you pass the Santa Fe Hotel and Casino; from there it's a six-mile drive on U.S. 95 to State Route 157. To get to 95 from the Las Vegas Strip, take either Tropicana, Flamingo, or Sahara west to Rainbow Boulevard. Turn right (north) onto Rainbow and watch for the sign for U.S. Highway 95 North.

If the trailhead is in Lee Canyon, take 95 north 21 miles past the Santa Fe and turn left (west) onto State Route 156. Lee Canyon lies at the end of 156. State Route 158 is a nine-mile road that begins along 157 and deadends into 156. Some of the trailheads are located on 158. To get to the hikes that originate at the Bonanza Trailhead, take 95 to Cold Creek Road. Go left (west) on Cold Creek Road for 16 miles until the road dead-ends into Bonanza Trailhead.

Red Rock Canyon

Red Rock Canyon, also called Red Rock Canyon National Conservation Area, encompasses 195,610 acres and is managed by the Bureau of Land Management (BLM). Red Rock Canyon is not part of the Mt. Charleston Area.

More than 1.5 million people visited Red Rock Canyon in 1996. Red Rock Canyon is best known for the Scenic Loop, a 13-mile, one-way, paved road that runs in a horseshoe shape around the canyon. You'll also find a Visitors Center with rangers, museum, books and maps, and restrooms, and a lifetime's worth of hiking, rock scrambling, bouldering, and climbing.

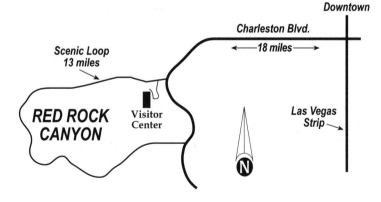

Directions to Red Rock Canyon

Getting to Red Rock is also easy. From the Las Vegas Strip, head west on Charleston Boulevard. Charleston becomes State Route 159 as you approach Red Rock Canyon. About 18 miles from Las Vegas Blvd., you'll see a "Welcome to Red Rock Canyon" sign. Turn right into Red Rock Canyon. At the toll booth you can drive onto the 13-mile one-way Scenic Loop road or go to the Visitors Center.

THE FORMAT OF THE HIKES

Every hike in this book is introduced by the format below.

Hike: Name of the hike and type of hike—up and back, closed loop, or open loop.

Trailhead: Location of the trailhead. The word "marked" if there's a sign identifying the trailhead.

Distance: One way or round trip. Noted in miles.

Elevation gain: How high the trail climbs. Expressed in feet.

Elevation peak: The height of the peak. Only hikes that go to a peak are listed.

Time: The time it takes an average hiker to complete the hike.

Difficulty: Scale of 1 to 5, where 1 is the easiest. This rating takes into consideration the distance, elevation gain, and the amount of class II or III climbing.

Danger level: Scale of 1 to 5, where 1 is the safest.

How easy to follow: Scale of 1 to 5, where 1 is a well-maintained trail and 5 is cross-country route.

Children: Designates whether it's safe for children (ages 5-11) to hike the trail with adults.

Map: Name of the applicable US topo map.

Directions: Explicit instructions on getting to the trailhead.

Overview: Summary of the hike, indicating whether the hike follows a trail, path, or route.

Comments: Interesting points and sights along the trail, warnings, and guidelines.

The Hike: The step-by-step guide to the trail, path, or route.

Trails, Paths, and Routes

The hikes in this book are classified as trails, paths, routes, or combinations of the three.

A trail is well-maintained and easy to follow. Trails in Red Rock are maintained by the Bureau of Land Management and have official trailhead signs. In Mt. Charleston, the Youth Correctional Facility maintains the trails, which also have trailhead signs.

A path is not maintained and might be hard to follow in certain spots. Paths have usually been created by hikers. They range in quality from being as distinct as a trail to being nearly impossible to follow due to lack of use. Paths sometimes begin along established trails, then splinter off to travel to a different destination. On some of the more obscure paths, cairns mark the way. On some of the more difficult hikes, I've endeavored to erect additional cairns. It's easier to follow an obscure path by looking ahead a few yards, rather than down at your feet.

A route is the least distinct of the three; no trail or path exists. A route is hiked by moving from one landmark to the next. All of the rock-scrambling and bouldering hikes in Red Rock are routes. With route hikes, it's necessary to remember distinctive landmarks on your way up. This is best done by turning around often so you can see what things will look like when you come back down. Routes appeal to hikers who are adventurous and like to figure out the best way to a landmark. All the canyon hikes in Red Rock are routes.

Many of the hikes are combinations of trails, paths, and routes. Any time a trail goes over rock for a distance, it becomes a route until the trail resumes. Many routes start from established trails. An example of a combination of the three is Mummy Mountain. It starts on the North Loop Trail, becomes a path above Mummy Springs, and turns into a route at the chute.

Just because a hike follows a route and not a trail doesn't mean it's easy to become lost. All of the bouldering hikes in the canyons of Red Rock are routes, but they're impossible to get lost on. All you have to do is turn around and hike out of the canyon.

Distance and Time

In the quick-reference feature that begins all the hikes, most of the "Distance" listings and "Time" estimates are based on a round trip for an "up and back" hike. An example is the Griffith Peak hike (pg. 22): the round trip distance is 10 miles, and it will take 6 to 7 hours to complete. "Closed loop" hikes start and end at the same place, so they're also assumed to be round trips. When I quote distance for an up and back or a closed loop as "one way," it's because there's much to explore at the trail's end, such as waterfalls or tanks. So although it might take you an hour to do the actual round-trip trek, you could spend several more hours messing around in the middle. "Open loops" have varying distances and times, since the main hike intersects another trail and can be done as an up and back or a loop. Distance and Time designations for open loops are based on the profile of the hike.

Danger Level

The danger-level rating takes into account the possibility of falling, altitude sickness, and potential weather situations. It's mandatory that you tell someone where you're going, what trail or route you plan to hike, and when you expect to return. You should always hike with at least one other person, but a party of four is preferred. In case of an accident, one hiker can stay with the victim and the other two can go for help. (See "Getting Lost or Stuck," p. 12.)

Climbing Grades

Class I—Hiking (Meonkopi, Bristlecone).
Class II—Hiking over rough terrain. The hands are used for balance (Oak Creek, South Sister).
Class III—Hiking and climbing using hands and feet. The rock is steep, though exposure is not significant (McFarland, Bridge).
Class IV—Climbing steep terrain. The exposure is significant and ropes are highly recommended.
Class V—Rock climbing. Technical climbing skills are a must.

The more you learn about climbing, the better prepared you'll be for the more difficult hikes discussed in this book.

Rock scrambling and bouldering can be dangerous and some of the hikes in Red Rock and Mt. Charleston require class III moves. Especially in Red Rock, but also in Mt. Charleston, hikers fall regularly, causing serious injury, sometimes resulting in death. Do not hike alone. Some of the hikes go to such remote areas, it could be days before another hiker would find you.

Maps

The hikes that follow trails have maps that provide a general overview of the hike. Most of the rock-scrambling and bouldering hikes do not have maps, since their usefulness would be minimal. Also note that the maps are not drawn to scale.

Every map follows the format below:

Main trail ···

Secondary trail —·—·—·—·—·—·—

Route — — — — — — — — — — — ·

Paved road ▬▬▬▬▬▬▬▬▬▬▬

Gravel road ————————————

US Highway ⑨⑤   State Highway ⑮⑦

Maps are not drawn to scale.

Compass Bearings

All compass bearings cited in the book are magnetic north. You don't have to account for declination. This keeps things simple and avoids the need for determining the declination for the Las Vegas area, then subtracting appropriately. The purpose of providing the bearings is to help guide you to the correct landmark. The bearings set the general direction; your common sense will allow you to locate the correct chute, gully, or peak.

FLORA

Many of the plants in the Southwestern desert and mountains can be used as landmarks while hiking. By being able to identify plants and trees, you can use them as markers to retrace your steps back to the trailhead. Because I've used plants and trees as landmarks in many of the hike descriptions, let's identify them.

bristlecone pine—Twisted, knotty pine found at elevations of 9,000 feet and above, with needles in clusters of five.
(desert) scrub oak—Spiny, many-branched, thicket-forming scrub; occasionally a small tree. Grows up to 20 feet tall. Leaves are irregularly shaped, with sharp pointy ends that tear clothing and skin.
juniper—A 15- to 30-foot-tall tree with scale-like leaves in clusters of three. They produce blue-black berries.
pinion pine—Short pine with short single needles on the twigs.
ponderosa pine—Towering trees that can grow up to 100 feet tall, with long needles in clusters of three and lots of bark. Normally found at higher elevations.
manzanita—Small shrub with red-barked branches and green non-spiny leaves.
yucca—Has a clustered trunk with very sharp, thick, bayonet-like leaves 18 to 24 inches long and white and purple flowers.

FAUNA

Red Rock and Mt. Charleston have a variety of animal life, but except for snakes, which are rarely seen or heard, the danger level from animals is almost non-existent. The remote hikes starting from Bonanza Trailhead in the Mt. Charleston Area offer the best chance of seeing larger animals. Some of the more interesting animals you might see while hiking are discussed below.

The mountain lion, also known as the cougar, puma, or panther, is the second largest North American cat. Mountain lions live up to 20 years and can weigh as much as 165 pounds.

They're found around the cliffs in Red Rock and in the mountain ranges of Mt. Charleston. Mountain lions are nocturnal. If you're lucky enough to see one, don't run; cats love to chase things. There have been only 13 deaths due to mountain lion attacks in the last 100 years in the western states.

Bighorn sheep are brownish-gray with heavy curling horns. They're one of the desert's most adaptive animals. These animals are amazing to watch as they run straight up the mountain slopes, sometimes leaping 20 feet from cliff to cliff. Herd sizes vary depending on the time of year, but normally contain less than a dozen. Since they live in remote areas, their exposure to people is limited, but they are not afraid of us. During the hot months they stay near water sources. One of the better places to get a glimpse of bighorn is deep in Oak Creek Canyon.

Pronghorn look like deer, only they're smaller, with black markings on their faces. They're often mistakenly thought to be part of the antelope family. They're about four-and-a-half feet long, with tails ranging from three to six inches, and black horns less than a foot long. They weigh from 80 to 105 pounds and travel in bands from a dozen to over 100. They're fast, and can be seen running at more than 40 mph out at Red Rock.

Desert mule deer are the most common large mammal found in southern Nevada. They're gray with a darker strip along their back and a black-tipped tail. Their large wide ears resemble the ears of a mule, which distinguishes them from other types of deer. Late in the day and at night are their active times. In Red Rock they are found among the thick growth along washes.

Burros are commonly seen along State Route 159 between Red Rock Canyon and Spring Mountain Ranch State Park, two miles west. They're tame and friendly, and will approach cars that park along the side of the highway to view them. You might be tempted to feed them, but it's not a good idea for the wild burros to get too dependent on handouts.

Wild horses (mustangs) are less common, but are occasionally spotted in the desert around Las Vegas. The BLM has a program where people can adopt wild horses or burros as pets. For info, call (702) 475-2222.

Snakes

Snakes are seldom seen or heard in Red Rock, and almost never in the Mt. Charleston Area. Most snakes in Red Rock and Mt. Charleston are not poisonous. Southern Nevada is home to only five poisonous snakes, all of them rattlesnakes. The most active months for snakes are April and May, and the most active times are early morning and evening. Luckily, rattlesnakes make a rattling sound to alert enemies before they come too close. If you hear this sound, walk in the opposite direction. In the 1,100 miles I hiked while preparing this book, I only heard two rattlesnakes, and I've never met anyone who was bitten by a snake while hiking. The rule of thumb is to pay attention to where you're placing your hands and feet.

CAUTIONS

Weather

Who said it's always sunny in Las Vegas? It is most of the time, but the "monsoon" season begins in mid-July and continues through August. Many days, Mt. Charleston starts with clear skies, only to give way to afternoon thunderstorms. These thunderstorms can be very dangerous; they're often accompanied by lightning and sometimes hail. Being on top of a mountain in a lightning storm is not fun! The trails often turn into streams, and walking in water increases your chances of being struck by lightning. Your best defense is to pay attention to the weather forecasts and begin your hikes early; many storms don't get going until after noon. Still, sometimes it's a tricky call. On many occasions I've been on a mountain when it looked certain that it would storm, only to have the dark clouds pass over without a drop of rain. Just use your common sense and watch the sky carefully.

Flash flooding is a serious problem at Red Rock. Normally, water encountered in the canyons is easily avoided by following paths leading around it. There's usually water in the creekbeds of Pine Creek, Oak Creek, and First Creek canyons. Although it rarely rains, when it does the canyons turn into raging rivers. Be careful if it looks like rain; each year people die from flash floods.

The Red Rock hiking season normally runs from mid-September to mid-May. Temperatures in the summer months exceed 100 degrees. If you hike Red Rock during the summer months, choose the short hikes and go early in the morning. Temperatures before 9 am rarely exceed 90 degrees. I've noted a few hikes that can be done during the summer months; however, most people hike Mt. Charleston during the summer.

Dehydration is a serious problem at Red Rock. If you're not acclimated to the desert climate, bring twice as much water as you think you'll need. A minimum of half a gallon for a four-hour hike is recommended. The old adage, "Drink before you get thirsty," is doubly important in the desert. Any water found on the hikes must be treated before drinking. Use a water filter or tablets to purify it.

THE TEN ESSENTIALS (PLUS ONE)

Since some of the hikes require climbing (class II and III), freedom of movement is important. Make sure your backpack isn't too restricting. Since all of the hikes are day hikes, little is needed besides the ten essentials: map, compass, flashlight, extra food, extra clothing, sunglasses, sunscreen (specific to southern Nevada), first-aid supplies, pocket knife, matches, and fire starter.

Getting Lost or Stuck

It's nearly impossible to get lost on the trails in Mt. Charleston. It's hard to get lost at Red Rock as well, but it does happen. The sandstone terrain looks amazingly similar and there are no trails across the sandstone, so finding your way down can be confusing. But there's always a safe way down; if you got up safely, you can get down safely. Remember to pay close attention to the landmarks and look back often to see what the view will look like when coming down. Using cairns on exploratory hikes is a good idea. Some people frown on the use of cairns, but they're helpful. A few cairns will help a hiker find his way back down and they can always be removed after you're done with them .

Though getting lost in Red Rock Canyon is difficult (you can almost always see a road, a trail, or the mouth of a canyon), getting stuck—winding up in a place from which you don't know the way down—is much more common. Some of the routes up the sandstone traverse multiple ledges. If you forget how you climbed up to a ledge, you might get stuck until you remember the way back down. If you follow the directions and study the photos in this book, turn around frequently, and pay attention to landmarks and cairns, you'll rarely have a problem. If you do get stuck, the first rule is: don't panic. Study the landscape carefully, then backtrack to the last place you recognize. You'll soon be back on track.

Stuck hikers have been known to call Search and Rescue by using their cell phones or yelling down to someone below. A stuck hiker who has Search and Rescue help him might be endangering a fallen hiker who needs them in a hurry. So only call as a last resort.

I'm not trying to scare anyone. Don't be so afraid of getting stuck that you refrain from venturing into the backcountry. Many hikes in this book are easy, safe, and follow well-marked trails. I have tried to detail a range of hikes. Anyone who starts with the easy hikes will gain confidence and want to progress. This book includes enough advanced hikes to satisfy those people who are looking for increasing challenges.

Hiking Etiquette

Most hikers go to the mountains to escape the problems of the city. Let's not bring those same problems to the mountains. Always practice no-trace hiking by using these guidelines.

1. Drive and ride (mountain bikes) only on roads and trails where such travel is allowed; hike only on established trails or paths, on rock, or in washes.

2. Help keep the area clean. Pack out your trash and recycle it, pick up trash even if it's not yours, and dispose of human waste properly. Bury all human waste at least 200 feet from the trail and at least six inches deep.

3. Protect and conserve desert water sources. Carry your own water. Leave pools, potholes, and running water undisturbed.
4. Allow space for wildlife. Teach children not to chase animals.
5. Leave historic sites, Native American rock art, ruins, and artifacts untouched for the future. Admire rock art from a distance. Stay out of ruins and report violations.

VOLUNTEERING

If you enjoy hiking in Red Rock or Mt. Charleston and want to volunteer your time and skills, there are a number of ways to do it.

In Red Rock
Adopt-a-Trail Program—This is a monthly trail clean-up open to any recognized group or organization. Contact the Volunteer Coordinator at the Visitors Center.

Individual Program—Individuals report on trail conditions. Contact the Volunteer Coordinator at the Visitors Center.

Friends of Red Rock—This is a not-for-profit corporation of volunteers who assist the BLM to protect the natural and cultural resources of the area. A number of volunteer positions are available. Call (702) 363-1922.

In Mt. Charleston
The contact person for all the following programs is Buddy Lyons at the U.S. Forest Service, (702) 873-8800.

Adopt-a-Trail Program—This is a monthly trail clean-up open to individuals.

Backcountry Ranger—Volunteers help patrol the high elevations during weekends and holidays. The emphasis is on trail surveys, fire prevention, and firefighting.

Campground Maintenance—Volunteers can help clean up the campgrounds in the Mt. Charleston Area.

Information/Education—Volunteers answer phones, provide visitor information, and assist in preparing informational literature.

Recreation Aid—Volunteers assist in daily operation and maintenance of recreational areas.

GROUP HIKING

Guide Services

Las Vegas Mountain Hikes—This company guides day hikes in Red Rock and Mt. Charleston. Guides supply everything you need, including: round-trip transportation, food, water, backpack, and an experience not soon forgotten. The author is one of the guides. For further information, call (702) 876-7926.

Jackson Hole Mountain Guides—This outfit offers guided technical climbs in Red Rock. For further information, call (702) 223-2176.

Clubs

Las Vegas Mountaineer's Club—This club offers hiking and climbing outings in the Spring Mountains and Red Rock Canyons at skill levels, ranging from beginner to technical (climbing). They also offer classroom and field instruction in equipment selection, map and compass use, first aid, snow climbing, and rock climbing. Contact the club at P.O. Box 36026, Las Vegas, NV 89133-6026, or call (702) 434-4323.

Sierra Club's Toiyabe Chapter—The largest and oldest hiking club in southern Nevada. Contact the club at P.O. Box 19777, Las Vegas, NV 89132, or call (702) 363-3267.

◆MT. CHARLESTON AREA◆

The Spring Mountains are the mightiest mountain range in southern Nevada, hemming in Las Vegas Valley on the west for 50 miles. The range gets its name from the 30 inches of precipitation that the high peaks grab from the moist winds that reach it from the Pacific Ocean and the Gulf of California. The 316,000-acre Spring Mountains National Recreation Area (SMNRA) is managed by the U.S. Forest Service; the centerpiece of the SMNRA is the Mt. Charleston Wilderness Area. Presiding over the Wilderness Area is Charleston Peak, which, at 11,918 feet, is the highest point in southern Nevada.

Charleston Peak

Charleston is the peak everyone wants to bag. Being above the timberline, it's the only treeless peak in the Mt. Charleston Area. At an almost 12,000-foot elevation and more than eight miles away by either of two trails, it's an all-day hike, and you'll have to choose your day carefully. The trails to the peak are not normally clear of snow until July, and by October the days are short and the temperature at the peak drops into the 30s. Your window to attempt the summit is further reduced by the August rainy season, which can make the hike dangerous.

You must prepare properly for Charleston Peak. Water, food, and comfortable hiking boots are mandatory. Rain gear and extra clothing should be in your backpack. Although Charleston is the Las Vegas-area peak to conquer, it's not overrun by hikers. Even in August (on a weekday), you might be the only hiker on the trail. This is all the more reason to be

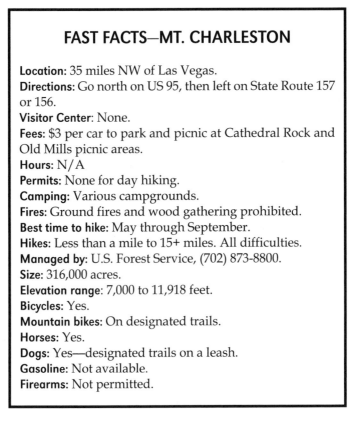

FAST FACTS—MT. CHARLESTON

Location: 35 miles NW of Las Vegas.
Directions: Go north on US 95, then left on State Route 157 or 156.
Visitor Center: None.
Fees: $3 per car to park and picnic at Cathedral Rock and Old Mills picnic areas.
Hours: N/A
Permits: None for day hiking.
Camping: Various campgrounds.
Fires: Ground fires and wood gathering prohibited.
Best time to hike: May through September.
Hikes: Less than a mile to 15+ miles. All difficulties.
Managed by: U.S. Forest Service, (702) 873-8800.
Size: 316,000 acres.
Elevation range: 7,000 to 11,918 feet.
Bicycles: Yes.
Mountain bikes: On designated trails.
Horses: Yes.
Dogs: Yes—designated trails on a leash.
Gasoline: Not available.
Firearms: Not permitted.

prepared and hike with at least one other person. There are no rangers, phones, or even manmade structures along the trail. If you get in trouble, you'll have to depend on your partner to help you.

The two trails to the peak are the South Loop and the North Loop trails. The signed trailhead for the South Loop Trail lies within the Cathedral Rock Picnic Area, about 30 yards south of the Cathedral Rock trailhead. The trail is well-maintained all the way to the peak.

The North Loop Trail is where the confusion begins. An out-of-print hiking book mistakenly referred to the North Loop as Trail Canyon and the mistake has caused some misunderstanding. The official North Loop Trail begins on State Route 158. It goes past a giant bristlecone pine known as "Raintree," and continues to the junction of Trail Canyon (it's a total of four miles from the trailhead to the junction). From the junction, the North Loop Trail is a straight shot to the peak. To add to the confusion, some maps and old-timers call the first part of the North Loop Trail (the part to Raintree) Deer Creek Trail. (State Route 158 is also called Deer Creek Highway.)

Trail Canyon, a two-mile trail that ends at the intersection with the North Loop Trail, offers a third trailhead for hiking

MT. CHARLESTON LODGE

The Mt. Charleston Bar and Restaurant, known to locals as the "Lodge," has served as the main gathering place for Mt. Charleston for almost 40 years. The 24-hour restaurant serves breakfast, lunch, and dinner. At the bar, you can enjoy your favorite libation a mile and a half above sea level. The Lodge also serves as a good landmark from high in the mountains; the circular driveway and green roofs of the cabins are hard to miss. The Lodge offers entertainment on the weekends and regularly throughout the summer.

The cabins are new additions to the Lodge. The first group opened in April 1995. When the rest are finished, there will be 24 cabins total. Each of the smaller 500-square-foot cabins contains a wooden king-sized bed, gas fireplace, loveseat, and Jacuzzi tub. Wooden floors, log walls, and the A-frame style give the feeling of a old-time log cabin. The distractions of the electronic world are absent. After relaxing indoors, you can sit on a swing on your private porch and take in the mountain view. The spacious 800-square-foot cabins offer all of the above, plus a second king-sized bed. Advance reservations are recommended. Call (702) 872-5408.

Charleston Peak. The signed trailhead for Trail Canyon is a half mile up Echo Drive. There's limited parking at the trailhead. If the parking area at the trailhead is full, park at Mary Jane Falls' parking lot a tenth of a mile back. Starting at Trail Canyon and intersecting the North Loop Trail is two miles shorter than starting at the North Loop trailhead; however, you'll encounter more elevation gain.

If you start the hike at Trail Canyon trailhead and return by the South Loop Trail, you don't need two cars; it's only a mile between the South Loop and Trail Canyon trailheads. This is the most popular way to hike Charleston Peak. If you start at North Loop trailhead (Deer Creek) and return via either Trail Canyon or South Loop, you will need two cars. These trailheads are 10 and 11 miles apart, respectively. Specific directions to each trailhead are furnished in the directions section for each hike. (See the North Loop, p. 68; South Loop, p. 44; and Trail Canyon, p. 34.)

Mummy Mountain

Mummy Mountain is one of the most recognizable mountains, and the second-highest peak, in the Mt. Charleston Area (elevation 11,514 feet). From US 95, what appear as three ski trails running down the mountain are really scree slopes. From State Route 156, you can see how the mountain got its name. Looking from left to right (south to north), it resembles the toe, tummy, and head of a mummy lying down. The mountain appears to have one continuous flat peak, but it doesn't. Upon closer inspection, you can see that the ridgeline is broken up into the toe, the tummy (main part), and the head. Each partition is separate and presents its own hiking challenge. Mummy Mountain can be done as a closed loop trail or an up-and-back hike.

Mummy Mountain can be deceiving, because it looks very different from different angles. For example, from Kyle Canyon the apparent ski slopes are not visible and the tummy is partially hidden; however, the pinnacles and the numerous saddles and chutes are visible from this angle.

Though Mummy Mountain is one of the most interesting peaks in the Charleston Area—the peak itself encompasses dozens of acres and offers much to explore—few people have hiked up to its summit. One reason for this is that from various points it looks impossible to hike without the use of ropes. Another reason: the few paths that lead up to the peak are not easily followed and no signs indicate that the paths take you to Mummy. The one trail that does go near Mummy Mountain leads to a different peak, and you have to look for a path that veers off toward Mummy. The route is covered on p. 62.

Griffith Peak

Griffith Peak lies to the south of Kyle Canyon and Charleston Peak. With an elevation of 11,072 feet, it's the third tallest peak in the Mt. Charleston Area. Griffith stands out as the only peak on the south side of Kyle Canyon that has a section of rock at the peak. The Griffith Peak Trail is one of the most popular hikes in Mt. Charleston. The views along the trail are unbelievable. To the ESE is the lush landscape of Harris Springs; it's strange to see greenery in the desert. La Madre Mountains, the mountains between Mt. Charleston and Red Rock, can be seen by looking to the southeast. A little farther south, the peaks of Turtlehead and Bridge Mountain in Red Rock Canyon come into view. Lovell Canyon can been seen by looking SSE. At Griffith Peak, you can look down on the Meadows, which lie to the NNW. You get a great view of Charleston Peak by looking up and to the NNW, and of the entire Kyle Canyon by looking north.

There are two trails to Griffith Peak. The Griffith Peak Trail (see p. 22) offers the great views to the SE, but requires a four-wheel-drive vehicle and an additional half-hour drive to the trailhead via Harris Springs Road. The other is the South Loop Trail to Mt. Charleston. Once at the ridgeline, a path splits off to the SE and goes up to Griffith Peak (see p. 40); however, you don't get the great views until you're standing on the summit.

DIFFICULTY INDEX

Okay, it's time to hike. This "Difficulty Index" will help you determine which hikes are best suited for your level of experience. If you're a first-timer, choose from the "Easy" category. If you have some experience (or are a first-timer with a high fitness level seeking more than an entry-level challenge), check out the "Moderate" category. Experienced hikers can go right to the "Difficult" hikes. A similar chart for Red Rock Canyon is found on p. 105. Happy hiking.

Easy	Moderate	Difficult
Fletcher Canyon: p. 26 Mary Jane Falls: p. 29 Big Falls: p. 31 Trail Canyon: p. 34 Echo Cave: p. 48 Robber's Roost: p. 56 Bristlecone: p. 79	Cathedral Rock: p. 37 Mummy Springs: p. 58 South Sister: p. 72 Mack's Peak: p. 75 Bonanza Peak: p. 90	Griffith Peak - Harris Springs Rd.: p. 22 Griffith Peak - South Loop: p. 40 South Loop: p. 44 Fletcher Peak: p. 51 Mummy Mountain: p. 62 North Loop: p. 68 Bonanza Trail: p. 81 McFarland: p. 84 Willow Peak: p. 94

♦ ♦ ♦

Griffith Peak via Harris Springs Road

Hike: Griffith Peak via Harris Springs Road — up and back
Trailhead: Harris Springs Road — marked
Distance: 10 miles — round trip
Elevation gain: 2,656 feet
Elevation peak: 11,056 feet
Time: 6 to 7 hours
Difficulty: 3
Danger level: 1
How easy to follow: 1
Children: no
Map: Griffith Peak, NEV

Directions: Take US 95 to State Route 157. Turn left on 157 and turn left on Harris Springs Road. Drive three miles and turn right at the fork. The road deadends at the trailhead. It's almost a half-hour drive on Harris Springs Road. A four-wheel-drive vehicle is recommended.

Overview: The **trail** heads west, then climbs a number of switchbacks to the base of the mountain. A short cross-country route to the top can be made from three different points on the trail.

Comments: Griffith Peak has the best views of any mountain in Mt. Charleston.

The Hike: The trail starts off at an easy pace as it makes its way west toward the saddle lying between Harris and Griffith peaks. There's a stunning view of Lovell Canyon to the south. The first part of the trail was once a road built by the Civilian Conservation Corps (CCC) in the 1940s. President Roosevelt

Griffith Peak

came to inspect the road and asked the foreman the road's destination. The foreman answered, "I don't know," and the President ordered the construction stopped. The road dead-ends, but the trail keeps going. If you look down to the south, you'll see an abandoned car at the bottom of a ravine. Apparently, someone thought the road went somewhere.

The trail keeps below and to the south of Harris Peak as it heads toward the saddle. (See Photo 1.) About an hour into

Photo 1

the hike, you can see rocky cliffs that compose the west part of the saddle. At the saddle, take a break and look NW for a view of Kyle Canyon. You won't need a long rest since the trail is very easy up to this point.

The incline increases as the trail begins to climb over the rocky cliffs SW of the saddle. The trail offers great views of Mummy Mountain, Kyle Canyon, and Mary Jane Falls by looking to the north. At the top of the switchbacks, you'll enjoy a great view of Kyle Canyon by walking over to—not off—the ledge.

The trail heads SW as it makes its way to the base of Griffith Peak. Red Rock Canyon can be seen by looking to the left (east). During the summer months a variety of flowers grows near the trail. Once at the top of the switchbacks, a hill off to the SW is often mistaken as Griffith Peak. Griffith lies behind this hill. The trail flattens out as it winds through an area that is still scarred from an old forest fire. Past the burnt area, the trail becomes steep as it heads south toward the peak. When the trail empties into a meadow, the first approach to the peak can be made. (See Photo 2.) This is a long and very steep approach. There are two hills to climb and then the peak. This approach is not recommended.

It's better to stay on the trail as it heads south and loops around the backside of Griffith. Soon a mostly barren bluff juts out to the east (left). This is your marker. As soon as the trail begins to pass the bluff, head west up to Griffith Peak. This

Photo 2

cross-country trek is hard, but short.

The easiest way to the summit is to stay on the trail until it reaches a crest. At this point, go north (right) and make your way to the peak. This route is less steep, but a bit longer, than the other two routes. If you're still on the trail and see Mt. Charleston Peak, you've gone too far. The trail continues on to Mt. Charleston; however, most hikers use the South Loop Trail to climb Mt. Charleston.

The wind and lower temperatures make Griffith Peak refreshing in the summer and cold in the winter. Millions of years ago the entire area was underwater. There are numerous fossils in the rocks at Griffith Peak. Look at them, but leave them so others can marvel at ancient history.

To Descend: Retrace your steps.

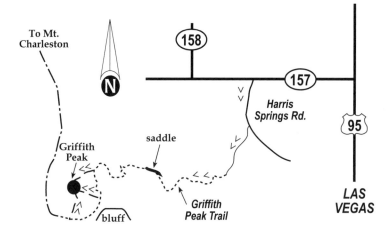

♦ ♦ ♦

Fletcher Canyon

Hike: Fletcher Canyon — up and back or open loop
Trailhead: North side of 157 — marked
Distance: 2 miles - 4 miles - 6.5 miles (car
shuttle required)
Elevation gain: 2,550 feet
Elevation peak: no peak
Time: 1 hour - 2 hours - 5 hours
Difficulty: 1 - 1 - 3
Danger level: 1 - 1 - 2
How easy to follow: 1 - 1 - 3
Children: yes - yes - no
Map: Charleston Peak, NEV

Directions: Take US 95 to State Route 157. The marked trailhead is a half mile past the intersection of 157 and 158 on the
right (north) side of 157. There is parking for one car at the
trailhead. Additional parking is available along the south side
of 157 at pulloffs located within 200 yards of the trailhead.

Overview: The **trail** follows a creekbed and goes into a canyon.

Comments: The trail starts out as an easy trek along the
mountainside. After a mile and a half, it winds through canyon walls 100 feet high. This hike is reminiscent of the canyon
hikes in Red Rock. The trail can be hiked as an easy 2-mile up
and back, 4-mile up and back, or 6.5-mile open loop. The bul-
letin board at the trailhead pertains only to the first mile of the
trail maintained by the Forest Service, which is why the length
of the trail is listed at one mile.

The Hike: The well-maintained trail heads north and offers a good view of rocky cliffs that lie in the distance. It then goes into a rocky wash and comes out on the far side. A number of less-maintained paths that branch off make interesting exploratory hikes for those who like the unknown. The first four miles of the trail has a slight grade that can be handled by a person of any fitness level. A large tree lies across a creekbed at the end of the one-mile maintained trail. Children can test their balancing skills by trying to walk across the tree. Although this marks the end of the one-mile maintained trail, the rest of the trail is easy to follow.

As the trail heads NW, cliffs on both sides begin to close in. Depending on the time of year and the previous winter's snowfall, the creekbed might contain running water. The trail crosses the creekbed a few times and splits, then rejoins a few hundred feet ahead. The canyon walls become tighter as the trail goes deeper into Fletcher Canyon. The trail turns craggy in spots as it winds around the wash and between the canyon walls. It turns south, empties into the creekbed, and weaves between 100-foot-tall canyon walls. The creekbed turns sharply to the north and boulder hopping becomes the best way to navigate. A steep trail veers off to the right toward a cave in the canyon wall, but you'll need ropes to climb into it.

Water may be flowing in parts of the creekbed as you continue through the slot canyon. Up ahead the creekbed divides. The right fork deadends in about 75 yards. A huge boulder, aptly named Obstacle Rock, blocks the entrance to the left fork of the creekbed. A small hole at the bottom-left corner provides a way past Obstacle Rock. It's a tight squeeze, and short people might need help to climb up and past Obstacle Rock. This might be the stopping point for beginners or hikers with children. From the trailhead to this point is about two miles.

Fifty yards past Obstacle Rock, the cliffs disappear, then it's easy going. Several paths follow the creekbed as it heads toward the North Loop Trail. Water flow might be heavy in some parts of the creekbed. The idea is to pick a path and follow it along the creekbed. The general direction is NW. As you follow the creekbed, you pass by a large tree that has been struck by lightning. Farther up, the creekbed turns into a wash and passes by whitish rock chips as it heads WNW (292 degrees). Stay in the main wash when a fork branches off to the left. The incline becomes moderate as the wash heads toward Mummy Mountain. The last half mile is steep as the wash heads toward the North Loop Trail.

Once at the North Loop Trail, head left (west) for about a third of a mile to the intersection with Trail Canyon Trail. Go left onto Trail Canyon Trail for two miles to its trailhead on Echo Drive Road. It's five miles from the Trail Canyon trailhead to the Fletcher Canyon trailhead. Using two cars, one parked at each trailhead, is recommended.

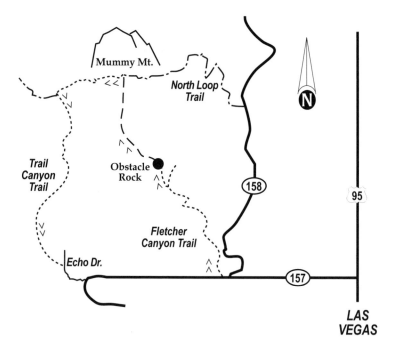

◆ ◆ ◆

Mary Jane Falls

Hike: Mary Jane Falls — up and back
Trailhead: Mary Jane Falls parking lot — marked
Distance: 1.2 miles — one way
Elevation gain: 900 feet
Elevation peak: 8,400 feet
Time: 1 to 2 hours
Difficulty: 2
Danger level: 1
How easy to follow: 1
Children: yes
Map: Charleston Peak, NEV

Directions: Take US 95 to State Route 157. Go left on 157 three miles past the intersection of 157/158 and turn onto Echo Drive at the hairpin turn. Drive just under a half mile and turn left at the sign for Mary Jane Falls. Drive a fifth of a mile on the gravel road to the parking lot. The trailhead is located at the far (north) side of the parking lot.

Overview: The **trail** climbs a series of steep switchbacks to the Falls.

Comments: This is a perfect hike for a beginner, a litmus test for those who want to find out if they'll like hiking. If you don't enjoy this trail, forget hiking. Mary Jane Falls is the most popular hike in Mt. Charleston.

The Hike: The trail begins at a leisurely pace, winding through ponderosa pines and aspens. As you head NW, the trail leads into a huge canyon. Looking south, you see the cliffs that hide

Big Falls, the most spectacular waterfall in Mt. Charleston. As you proceed up the trail, Big Falls comes into view. The dozen or more switchbacks take you up to and along the north canyon wall. The trail continues to climb, then heads directly toward Mary Jane Falls.

There's much to explore at the Falls. A cave behind the Falls lets you look out through the waterfall into the canyon below. Use caution scrambling up to the cave. The wet rocks are slippery and each year people get hurt or stuck at Mary Jane Falls. A second cave above the falls is impossible to reach without technical climbing experience and ropes. The waterfall flows year round, but it's heaviest in spring when the snow melts. There's another cave about 100 yards farther down the trail. This part of the trail is easy to navigate. Coming back down takes about half of the time of hiking up.

To Descend: Retrace your steps.

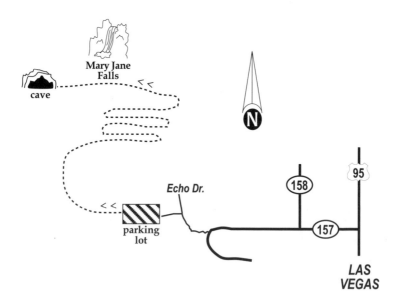

♦ ♦ ♦

Big Falls

Hike: Big Falls — up and back
Trailhead: Mary Jane Falls parking lot — marked
Distance: 1.75 miles — one way
Elevation gain: 800 feet
Elevation peak: 8,300 feet
Time: 1 hour
Difficulty: 2
Danger level: 2
How easy to follow: 2
Children: yes
Map: Charleston Peak, NEV

Directions: Take US 95 to State Route 157. Go left on 157 three miles past the intersection of 157/158 and turn onto Echo Drive at the hairpin turn. Drive just under a half mile and turn left at the sign for Mary Jane Falls Trail. Drive a fifth of a mile on the gravel road to the parking lot. The trailhead is located at the far (north) side of the parking lot.

Overview: After leaving Mary Jane Falls **trail**, the **route** heads SW into a wash and ends at Big Falls.

Comments: Big Falls is the most spectacular waterfall in Mt. Charleston. The flow rate is highest in the spring. The first half mile of the hike follows the Mary Jane Falls Trail.

The Hike: The trail begins at a leisurely pace as it winds through ponderosa pines and aspens. As you head NW, the trail leads into a huge canyon. Looking to the left, you see cliffs that hide Big Falls. As the trail veers to the right, two other

Photo 1

routes emerge. (The old route to Mary Jane Falls, now blocked by logs, lies to the left.) This is the route that leads to Big Falls. (See Photo 1.)

The route to Big Falls starts with a gentle incline as it heads SW toward a wash. It crosses over two fallen trees before it

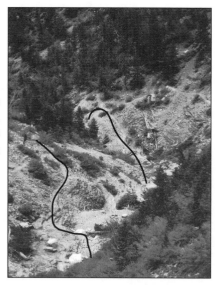

Note: Black lines are paths around obstacles. Line on left side shows alternative route when water is in the wash.

Photo 2

descends into the wash. A path to the west follows the entire wash. This is the course if you don't like boulder hopping or if the wash is filled with water. Once in the wash, it's up to you to pick the best route. Negotiating the wash requires a series of Class I and Class II boulder hopping. When you come to the large boulder blocking the wash, look for a path that goes up the left side of the wash. This path forks into upper and lower paths. Both paths go around the boulder and then descend back into the wash. (See Photo 2.) After descending back into the wash, it's a short trek to Big Falls.

Once at the falls, you have a variety of options: cool off in the water, eat lunch, or climb to the top of a bluff to catch a view of the wash. For the adventurous, a route to the far left of the falls leads to the top.

To Descend: Retrace your steps.

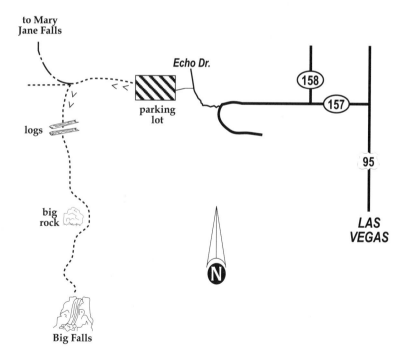

◆ ◆ ◆

Trail Canyon

Hike: Trail Canyon — up and back or open loop
Trailhead: Trail Canyon — marked
Distance: 2 miles — one way
Elevation gain: 1,523 feet
Elevation peak: no peak
Time: 1 hour
Difficulty: 1
Danger level: 1
How easy to follow: 1
Children: yes
Map: Charleston Peak, NEV

Directions: Take US 95 to State Route 157. Go left onto 157 and turn onto Echo Drive at the hairpin turn. Drive half a mile to the trailhead sign for Trail Canyon. There is limited parking at the trailhead.

Overview: The **trail** follows a drainage into a canyon and intersects the North Loop Trail.

Comments: This trail causes more confusion than any other trail in the Mt. Charleston Area. It is often mistakenly called the North Loop Trail (because it meets up with the North Loop Trail two miles from the trailhead). From the junction of those two trails you have three destination options.

The Hike: The trail starts off in a northerly direction at a leisurely pace, paralleling a dry creekbed that lies to the west. The trail winds through thick groves of aspens as it heads toward the North Loop Trail junction. To the east lies the rocky cliffs of Cockscomb Ridge. About a half mile into the hike, the North Rim Ridge can be seen by looking to the NW. Straight ahead lies the backside of Mummy Mountain.

The grade becomes moderate as the trail switches back through pinion pines. Five steps made out of logs help you climb toward the North Loop Trail. Just past this point, Charleston Peak can be seen by looking to the left. The trail flattens out briefly, then climbs a small hill as it heads due east toward Cockscomb Ridge. From this point, it's about 100 yards to the junction of Trail Canyon and North Loop Trail. (See Photo 1.)

Once at the junction, a number of options are available. You can go right and follow a path that runs along the Cockscomb Ridge. This path is about a mile in length and offers great views of Kyle Canyon. You can go left onto the North Loop Trail to Mt. Charleston. This should not be done on a whim. The weather at the peak can be severe any time of the year. (See the North Loop to Charleston Peak hike for a description.) A third option is to go straight onto the North Loop Trail to Raintree, a giant bristlecone pine, which is the oldest living thing in southern Nevada. It's about a mile and a half from the junction, with plenty of steep switchbacks.

Charleston Peak

To: Charleston Peak

From: Trail Canyon trailhead

To: Cockscomb Ridge

Photo 1

North Loop to Raintree

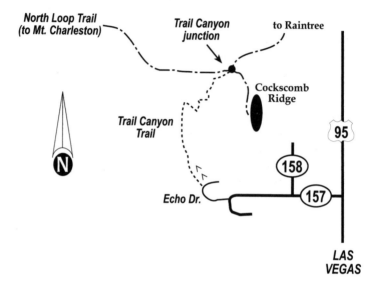

North Loop Trail
(to Mt. Charleston)

Trail Canyon
junction

to Raintree

Cockscomb
Ridge

95

Trail Canyon
Trail

158

157

N

Echo Dr.

LAS
VEGAS

♦ ♦ ♦

Cathedral Rock

Hike: Cathedral Rock — up and back
Trailhead: 1. Cathedral Rock Picnic Area — marked
        2. Before Cathedral Rock Picnic Area, top
        of the steps — marked
Distance: 3 miles — round trip (from the picnic area);
2.5 miles — round trip (from before the picnic area)
Elevation gain: 1,000 feet
Elevation peak: 8,600 feet
Time: 2.5 hours
Difficulty: 2
Danger level: 1
How easy to follow: 1
Children: yes
Map: Charleston Peak, NEV

Directions: Take US 95 to State Route 157. Go left on 157, drive past the hairpin turn, and turn right into Cathedral Rock Picnic Area. (See Photo 1.) The trailhead is on the west side of the road, a few yards past the fee booth. The entrance fee is $3 per car. Parking is available across from the trailhead; however, it may be full on weekends. An alternative trailhead is on 157 about a half mile past the hairpin turn on the west side of the road. Parking and restrooms are located near the trailhead. A concrete stairway leads to the trailhead.

Overview: The **trail** starts off easy, flattens out, then becomes steep before reaching the peak.

Comments: Cathedral Rock, the second most popular trail in Mt. Charleston, is a good hike for beginners. You can see Cathedral Rock, the huge pinnacle that looms above the Mt. Charleston Lodge, by looking at the (imaginary) 10 o'clock position as you approach the hairpin turn on 157. (See Photo 2.) From the peak, you enjoy fantastic views of the Lodge and parts of Kyle Canyon.

Photo 1

The Hike: From the picnic area, the trail starts off in a westward direction at a slight grade that anyone can handle. It winds through thick patches of aspens and evergreens before intercepting the alternative trail. The trail turns south and heads toward the magnificent Echo Cliffs, which have a sheer drop of almost 800 feet. As the trail snakes to the west of Echo Cliffs, a side trail leads to a small seep. Water flows almost year round, making the 100-yard walk worth the effort.

Cathedral Rock

Photo 2

Once past Echo Cliffs, the trail heads west and the grade becomes steeper as it makes its way up to a saddle. Once at the saddle, you can see the destruction an avalanche can wreak on a mountain. Many trees and boulders are still misplaced by an avalanche that occurred years ago.

The trail flattens out as it heads toward the backside of Cathedral Rock. This is the easiest and most enjoyable part of the trail, a cakewalk through a forest, and you forget that you re 8,000 feet above sea level. When the trail divides, take the right fork.

Save your energy for the last quarter mile of the trail it s steep. About a half-dozen switchbacks take you to the top of Cathedral Rock. Once on top the view becomes more spectacular with every step. On the far NE side, there s a place to sit and admire the view. Just below is the Mt. Charleston Lodge and farther to the east you can see the desert floor. To the north is Mummy Mountain, to the NW is Mary Jane Falls, and to the west is Charleston Peak.

If you eat lunch, you may have a visitor or two. This is the only place in the world you ll have the opportunity to see the Palmer chipmunk. As hard as it is, resist feeding them. Feeding them causes the chipmunks to become dependent on humans for their food. In the winter the chipmunks must rely on their food-gathering skills, or perish. Watch children closely at the top; the drop-offs are more than 100 feet at the edges. Railings have been erected, but they seem to induce people to climb down to them, which brings them even closer to the edge.

The other trailhead (by the restrooms) starts out with a moderate incline and continues to climb until it intercepts the main trail. This course is shorter, but a little more difficult.

To Descend: Retrace your steps.

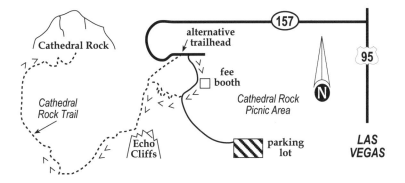

♦ ♦ ♦

Griffith Peak
(South Loop Trail)

Hike: Griffith Peak (South Loop Trail) — up and back
Trailhead: Cathedral Rock Picnic Area — marked
Distance: 9.5 miles — round trip
Elevation gain: 3,470 feet
Elevation peak: 11,056 feet
Time: 5 to 6 hours
Difficulty: 3
Danger level: 1
How easy to follow: 1
Children: yes
Map: Charleston Peak, NEV and Griffith Peak, NEV

Directions: Take US 95 to State Route 157. Turn left on 157 and follow it to Cathedral Rock Picnic Area. (See Photo 1.) The trailhead is located a tenth of a mile past the fee booth on the right (west) side of the road. Parking is available at various spots along the road. If Cathedral Rock Picnic Area is full or closed, parking is available just before entering the picnic area.

Overview: The **trail** climbs a number of switchbacks to the ridgeline. From the ridgeline it's a short but steep hike to Griffith Peak.

Comments: Griffith Peak offers one of the best views in the Mt. Charleston Area. Unlike the Harris Springs Road approach, this trail does not require a four-wheel-drive vehicle to get to the trailhead.

The Hike: The South Loop Trail starts off at an easy pace as it heads in a SSW direction. The grade increases rapidly as the trail turns east and passes to the east of Echo Cliffs. The trail winds through ponderosa pines and white furs, along with smaller aspens that are colorful during the fall. As the trail turns SW, it passes through Echo Cliffs. A small cave is

Griffith Peak

located near the bottom of Echo Cliffs. Off to the south is Springs Fork where water flows year round. It's a short quarter-mile trek to the Springs. The trail climbs a series of moderate switchbacks up the backside of Echo Cliffs. There's a great overlook at the top of Echo Cliffs. Kyle Canyon, Mummy Mountain, and Cathedral Rock are all in view. The overlook is two miles from the trailhead.

The trail leaves the overlook in a westerly direction with a

Photo 1

Mummy Mt.

gradual incline. About ten minutes into this segment of the hike, you'll see a wooden sign indicating mountain bikes are not allowed. The trail crosses a drainage and starts a series of moderate switchbacks that take you to the South Rim Plateau. Many of the switchbacks on the north end offer great views of Kyle Canyon, Cathedral Rock, and Mummy Mountain. (See Photo 2.)

Photo 2

The landscape changes into a meadow before reaching the plateau. The last quarter mile is steep, but offers a good view of Griffith Peak. Upon reaching the South Rim, a sign indicates the distances to Charleston Peak, Harris Saddle, and back to Kyle Canyon—the trailhead. Griffith Peak is not listed. The elevation is 10,700; the distance is four miles.

Go left onto the trail and head toward Griffith Peak. In about 400 yards the trail divides. The path to the left goes up to Griffith Peak. (See Photo 3.) This is a short hard path climbing more than 300 feet to the peak. The trail goes around, not up to, Griffith Peak and back down to Harris Saddle. The wind and lower temperatures make Griffith Peak refreshing in the summer and cold in the winter. Millions of years ago the entire area was underwater

Photo 3

and there are numerous fossils in the rocks at Griffith Peak. Look at them, but leave them so others can marvel at ancient history.

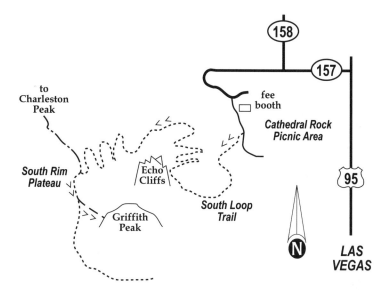

♦ ♦ ♦

South Loop to Charleston Peak

Hike: South Loop to Charleston Peak — up and back or open loop
Trailhead: Cathedral Rock Picnic Area — marked
Distance: 8.5 miles — one way
Elevation gain: 4,190 feet
Elevation peak: 11,918 feet
Time: 4 to 6 hours
Difficulty: 5
Danger level: 2
How easy to follow: 1
Children: no
Map: Charleston Peak, NEV

Directions: Take US 95 to State Route 157. Go left on 157, pass the hairpin turn, and turn right into Cathedral Rock Picnic Area. (See Photo 1 in the Cathedral Rock hike, p. 37.) The trailhead is located one-tenth of a mile past the fee booth on the right (west) side of the road. The entrance fee is $3 per car. Parking is available across from the trailhead; however, the lot may be full on weekends. If the parking areas are full or closed, parking is also available just before entering the picnic area on the right (west) side of the road. It's a quarter-mile walk to the trailhead from the entrance to Cathedral Rock Picnic Area.

Overview: The **trail** follows a number of switchbacks leading to a ridgeline. From the ridgeline, the trail weaves through a meadow before the final approach to the peak.

Comments: This trail takes you to Mt. Charleston Peak. Once you reach the grassy wonderland, the hiking becomes easy. If you're into camping, this is one of the best spots in all of Mt. Charleston. The last half mile is very strenuous, but the view from the peak makes it all worthwhile.

The Hike: The South Loop Trail starts off at an easy pace as it heads in a SSW direction. The grade increases rapidly as the trail turns easterly and passes to the east of Echo Cliffs. As the trail turns back to a SW direction, it passes through Echo Cliffs. To the south is Springs Fork, where water flows year round. It's a short quarter-mile trek to the Springs.

The trail follows a series of moderate switchbacks as it climbs up the backside of Echo Cliffs. There's a great overlook at the top of Echo Cliffs (two miles from the trailhead); Kyle Canyon, Mummy Mountain, and Cathedral Rock can be viewed from this overlook.

The trail leaves the overlook and takes a westerly direction with a gradual incline. It crosses a drainage and starts a series of moderate switchbacks that take you up to the South Rim Plateau. Many of the switchbacks on the north end offer grand views of Kyle Canyon, Cathedral Rock, and Mummy Mountain. The landscape starts to change into a meadow before reaching the plateau. The last quarter mile is steep, but it offers a good view of Griffith Peak. Upon reaching the plateau, a sign indicates the distances to Charleston Peak, Harris Saddle, and back to Kyle Canyon (the trailhead). The elevation is 10,700 feet; the distance to this point is four miles.

The trail heads westerly and soon enters into a meadow. This three-mile segment of the trail is referred to as "The Meadows" and is a favorite spot for campers. Upon closer inspection there is an upper and lower meadows. The grade is slight with plenty of downhill treks. Charleston Peak comes into view several times during the ramble through The Meadows.

The Meadows gives way to a grove of timber. The trail heads due west and the grade picks up slightly in this wooded area. It hugs the ridgeline for more than half a mile, offering remarkable views of Kyle Canyon, Mt. Charleston Lodge, and State Route 157. Directly across is Mummy Mountain and to the left is the North Ridge Rim.

The trail turns away from the ridgeline and heads SW before it climbs to another ridge. Off to the left is an unnamed peak that many hikers mistake for Mt. Charleston. The trail rises to the saddle and Mt. Charleston ridgeline comes into view. The trail heads to the right (NW) toward Mt. Charleston and away from the false peak. A path to the left leads down to Peak Springs. It's a very tough one-mile trek down to the Springs, but the Springs flows year round, in case you're low on water.

Due to the wind and elevation, the landscape becomes harsh; the bristlecone pines are reduced to twisted dwarfs. You're higher than 11,000 feet at this point, but luckily the incline is moderate. Charleston Peak looks more like a ridgeline than a summit from this angle. Just off the trail to the right are the remains of a 1955 plane crash, which have never been cleared away. Hikers have taken the smaller pieces of the wreckage as souvenirs.

The last half mile to the peak is a steep 20% grade. Just before the peak, the trail splits. Both trails go to the peak; however the trail to the left is less steep. The wind can be harsh up here above the treeline. It's important to drink plenty of water before this final ascent. One cause of altitude sickness is a lack of water.

Congratulations! You're standing, or lying down questioning your sanity, at the highest point in southern Nevada. Take a moment to experience the silence, breathe the clean air, and be thankful you're in good enough shape to have made it to this peak. The peak offers a fantastic 360-degree view of southern Nevada, eastern California, and southern Utah. An Army box contains a sign-in book. A dug-out fort that holds 10 people is a favorite resting point before starting back down. You can return the way you came up or make a loop by hiking down the North Loop Trail to Trail Canyon. (See the North Loop and Trail Canyon hikes for more information.)

If you parked at the South Loop trailhead, hiked to the peak, and plan to come down North Loop Trail to Trail Canyon, there's a shortcut to your car. Walk down Echo Drive, passing the Mary Jane Falls' sign, to a parking lot on the right. A sign indicates this is a temporary trail to Cathedral Rock. Follow this broad trail to the parking lot just outside Cathedral Rock Picnic Area. Go through Cathedral Rock Picnic Area to the South Loop trailhead. This shortens the walk between the trailheads by a half mile.

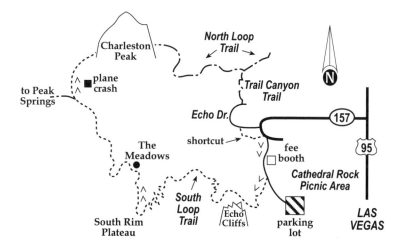

♦ ♦ ♦

Echo Cave

Hike: Echo Cave — up and back
Trailhead: End of Cathedral Rock Picnic Area
Distance: 3 miles — round trip
Elevation gain: 400 feet
Elevation peak: none
Time: 2 hours
Difficulty: 2
Danger level: 2
How easy to follow: 1
Children: yes
Map: Charleston Peak, NEV

Directions: Take US 95 to State Route 157. Go left on 157 into Cathedral Rock Picnic Area. Stay on the main street until it deadends into a parking lot. At the far end of the parking lot a paved path marks the start of the hike. (See Photo 1.)

Photo 1

Overview: The **trail** heads toward Echo Cliffs, connects with the South Loop Trail, then makes a short trek to a cave.

Comments: This is one of numerous caves located in Mt. Charleston. The hike offers many options and is a good choice if you're unsure how far you want to hike.

The Hike: Follow the unmarked paved pathway for about 50 yards and go right onto a gravel trail that heads south. Stay on the trail, passing a trail that comes in from the right. Just beyond that point, the trail comes to a T-type intersection. Go right and follow the trail as it narrows, goes up a hill, then widens at the top. Look to the left for a good view of Echo Cliffs at this point. The trail narrows, leads up an incline, and connects with a wider trail. Going left takes you to the cave; going right takes you back to the first turnoff you passed. If you go right, making a loop out of this part of the hike, go left when you intersect the lower part of the trail. This course takes

Photo 2

you back to the trailhead; the distance is about three-quarters of a mile.

Continuing toward the cave, the trail passes an avalanche area before connecting with the South Loop Trail. Go left onto the South Loop Trail. The cave becomes visible as the trail winds past Echo Cliffs. The cave sits at the base of Echo Cliffs. Once on the switchbacks, a number of paths lead toward the cave. These paths disappear, but with the cave in sight it's easy to make your own route. Once near the cave, a ledge forms and leads toward the cave. Hike parallel to the ledge until you find an easy climb up to the ledge. The cave is about 15 yards away at this point. Continue on the ledge until it goes underneath the cave. It's a short climb (class III) to the cave. (See Photo 2.) The cave is 15 feet long and offers a good place to relax before planning your next adventure.

From this point you can hike back to the South Loop Trail and continue up it to various points, return to Cathedral Rock Picnic Area via the South Loop Trail, or retrace your steps to the parking lot.

To Descend: Retrace your steps.

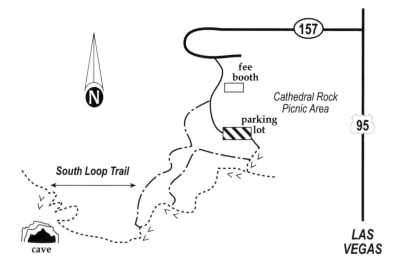

♦ ♦ ♦

Fletcher Peak

Hike: Fletcher Peak via Hummingbird Hollow — up and back or open loop
Trailhead: State Route 158 across from the 3-mile marker
Distance: 6.6 miles — round trip
Elevation gain: 2,544 feet
Elevation peak: 10,319 feet
Time: 4 to 5 hours
Difficulty: 3
Danger level: 2
How easy to follow: 4
Children: no
Map: Angel Peak, NEV

Directions: Take US 95 to State Route 157. Turn left on 157. Turn right onto 158 and go three miles to a small gravel pulloff on the left side of the road. A three-mile marker is on the right side of the road. (See Photo 1.)

Overview: The **route** is a scramble up the canyon. It follows a dry creekbed to a saddle. From the saddle the route travels along the ridgeline to the peak. Photo 2 shows an overview of the canyon.

Comments: This is a great hike for someone who wants to rock-scramble in Mt. Charleston. Fletcher Peak offers good views of Kyle Canyon.

The Hike: The arrow in Photo 1 shows the start of the gravel path. After 50 yards turn left onto a narrow dirt and gravel path and head south (210 degrees) up Hummingbird Hollow Canyon. The route becomes rocky as it weaves between cliffs. A few paths have developed along parts of the canyon. It's up to you to determine which path offers the easiest way to get to the top of the canyon. The paths either lie at the bottom of the canyon or travel along the right or left sides. The latter requires more climbing. The route continues at a steep pace. A

Photo 1

number of dead-looking trees stand near the top of the canyon. (See Photo 3.) In late July or August you can munch on gooseberries and elderberries along the route.

When the path divides near the top of the canyon, the route goes to the left. The path that leads to the right eventually deadends into cliffs. There is a good deal of class II rock scrambling at this point. After the class II section, the path flattens out. A fallen tree, about four feet off the ground, blocks the path. Beyond it, the path follows close to the left side of the canyon wall. Watch out for low-hanging branches (they hurt). Depending on the amount of snowfall from the previous winter and the time

Photo 2

of year, water might be flowing in the creekbed the path follows. The cliffs disappear as the path reaches the summit and starts up a dry creekbed. A short side path that branches off to the right goes to the top of Hummingbird Hollow. A fantastic view of the canyon you've just hiked is your reward for making it to this point. (See Photo 3.) Take a break and relax after the taxing climb.

Follow the path that heads SSW (250 degrees) into the creekbed. The slope is gentle and the rocky path turns into soft dirt with pine cones covering the ground. Another creekbed splits off to the left, but stay in the one you've been hiking. Soon, talus can be seen on the right side of a steep slope. The creekbed makes a sweeping left and heads SW (210 degrees). Ponderosa pines and white firs shade the path as it heads toward the saddle, then cuts through a rocky area. A separate route veers off to the right along the rock. When the path becomes hard to follow, stay to the left of the gravel slope where it's easier to follow.

The path becomes steeper as it winds through the small rocky outcroppings and bends to the south (190 degrees) as it

Arrows indicate dead trees.

Photo 3

makes its way to the saddle. When it turns rocky, it requires a little bit of class II climbing. The creekbed divides. Both routes take you to Fletcher Peak, but the creekbed to the left is steeper and the path in this creekbed is harder to follow. Do not take the left fork. A few minutes after hiking past the divide, the saddle comes into view. Mummy's Toe can be spotted by looking a little to the right of the saddle. Again, the creekbed divides; both routes take you to Fletcher Peak. Once more, it's easier to stay in the main creekbed. The creekbed becomes steeper as it comes to the saddle.

At the saddle the route intersects a path. Heading left on the path takes you to Fletcher's Peak; heading right takes you to the North Loop Trail. At the saddle Griffith Peak is due south (180 degrees), Mummy's Toe is to the NW (312 degrees), and Raintree is to the NW about a half mile away.

From this saddle the faint path to Fletcher Peak heads east (84 degrees) and stays just below and to the west of the ridgeline. At the top of the first hill, Fletcher Peak lies SE (130 degrees). The path goes to another small saddle, then stays about 25 yards left (east) of the new ridgeline. The path is very faint. Continue heading toward Fletcher Peak and you'll pick it up again. There's a great view of Charleston Peak at the top of this second hill—look to your right. The path goes over rock, then turns east for the final leg to Fletcher Peak. The path disappears among rock slabs, but with the peak in sight, it's impossible to miss it. You'll find a plastic jar with a sign-in book inside the cairn that marks the peak. Fletcher Peak offers one of this elevation's best views of Kyle Canyon, Griffith Peak, Harris Peak, and even parts of Red Rock.

Fletcher has two peaks; the second is a 10-minute walk to the SE. You can see it from the peak you're on; it's a little lower in elevation.

To Descend: Keep Mummy's Toe in front of you. At the first ridgeline, the trail lies about 25 yards to the east. Go to the west of the final rock outcropping and down into the saddle where the creekbed ended. From this point you can either go down into the creekbed and back the way you came up, or follow the faint path NW (308 degrees) that connects to the

North Loop Trail. This connecting path, about a half mile long, becomes easy to follow after the first 100 yards. At the junction of North Loop Trail, go right (east) down the trail to the trailhead. The trail terminates at the North Loop trailhead on State Route 158. It's about a two-mile hike back to Fletcher Peak trailhead.

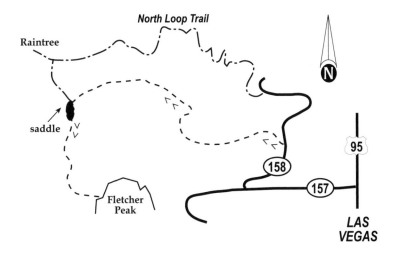

♦ ♦ ♦

Robber's Roost

Hike: Robber's Roost — up and back
Trailhead: On State Route 158 — marked
Distance: less than a half mile — round trip
Elevation gain: 200 feet
Elevation peak: no peak
Time: 30 minutes
Difficulty: 1
Danger level: 2
How easy to follow: 1
Children: yes
Map: Angel Peak, NEV

Directions: From US 95 turn left on State Route 157. Turn right on State Route 158 and follow it for 3.4 miles to a paved parking lot on the right (east) side of the road. The trail begins across from the parking lot.

Overview: The **trail** climbs a steep hill to a cave-like structure.

Comments: This cave, according to local legend, was a hideout for Mexican bandits when they made their raids into southern Nevada and Utah.

The Hike: From the trailhead, head west up the gravel trail toward the limestone cliffs. The grade is strenuous, but short. Caution is urged, due to the steepness and slippery gravel on the trail. Once at the rocky cliffs there's much to explore and climb. Who knows, you might find some loot hidden by the Mexican bandits!

To Descend: Retrace your steps.

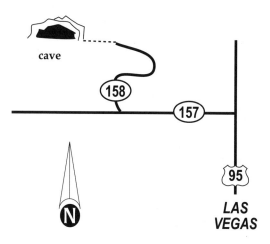

Mummy Springs

Hike: Mummy Springs — up and back
Trailhead: On State Route 158 — marked
Distance: 7 miles — round trip
Elevation gain: 1,100 feet
Elevation peak: no peak
Time: 3.5 to 4.5 hours
Difficulty: 2
Danger level: 1
How easy to follow: 1
Children: yes
Map: Charleston Peak, NEV

Directions: Take US 95 to State Route 157. Turn left on 157 and turn right onto State Route 158. Travel five miles to the North Loop trailhead sign, located on the left (west) side of the road. (See Photo 1.)

Overview: The **trail** climbs gently to a plateau. After a number of moderately steep switchbacks, it peaks out and gradually descends 150 feet over the next third of a mile to Raintree. Mummy Springs is an easy half mile farther.

Comments: This is an easy hike that passes a 3,000-year-old bristlecone pine, the oldest living thing in the region. The tree has been named "Raintree." The trail is the starting point for many hikes and is one of the trails that leads to Charleston Peak.

The Hike: The trail starts off at an easy grade, wandering past ponderosa pine, pinion pine, and mountain mahogany. From

North Loop
Trail sign

Photo 1

June through September, a number of colorful flowers grow
alongside the trail. To the east on Angel Peak rests a large,
white, ball-shaped observatory. This can be used as a landmark. The trail has a few moderate switchbacks before reaching a plateau. Pause at the plateau for a good view to the NE.
Several bristlecone pines are scattered throughout this area,
indicating you're above 9,000 feet. About 100 yards before the
trail starts to ascend, a faint path heads NW. This is the "Wild
Horse" path and is used to make a partial loop out of the hike.
(See Photo 2.)

After 12 moderately steep switchbacks, the trail climbs to
its highest elevation (10,200 feet). It then descends 150 feet over
the next third of a mile. Glimpses of Mummy Mountain can be
seen by looking west and the limestone cliffs of Mummy's Toe
hover directly in front of the trail.

Finally, you come to Raintree, the giant and ancient bristlecone pine. It's amazing to think that when this living plant
was a seedling, the Roman Empire was still centuries in the
future. Raintree acts as a dividing point. A wooden sign next
to it indicates your options and the distances. You can stop,
eat lunch, and admire Raintree; you can follow the trail to

Mummy Springs; or you can continue another eight miles to Charleston Peak. Water trickles year round from the seep at Mummy Springs. It's well worth the extra half-mile hike from Raintree, and a great place to have lunch. It's often very windy at Raintree; however, Mummy Springs is protected from the wind, making it a perfect place to eat.

Don't hike to Charleston Peak unless you're prepared. The peak is another eight miles from this point. It takes an additional 6 to 10 hours and the temperature rarely exceeds 60 degrees at the peak. The rest of the way to the peak is for experienced hikers only.

You can make a partial loop out of this hike by taking the Wild Horse path back to Highway 158. First descend the 12 switchbacks, till you come to the plateau. The faint Wild Horse path branches off from the main trail and heads west. Follow the path through the trees. When the path ends, head north toward a gravel road seen in the distance. The road is only a landmark; you won't reach it. Eventually, you'll be on a ridge that overlooks cabins in the valley below. Follow the ridgeline east for about three-quarters of a mile, then head south off the ridge down into a drainage. The ridge and drainage run paral-

Mummy Mt.

Wild Horse Path   **Photo 2**

lel, making it easy to find the drainage. Once in the drainage, head east and follow it to another gravel road. Go right on this gravel road for 30 yards to Highway 158. Head right (south) on 158 for a quarter mile to the North Loop trailhead.

Another alternative is to continue on the North Loop Trail from Raintree to the Trail Canyon Trail and descend down to Echo Drive. This is an interesting six-plus-mile hike, but must be done with a car at each trailhead. The drive from North Loop trailhead to Trail Canyon trailhead is about 10 miles.

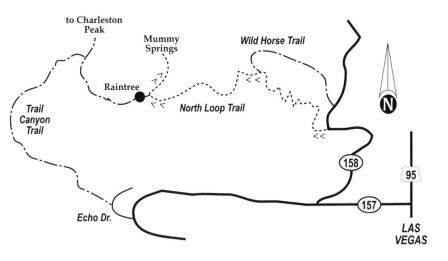

♦ ♦ ♦

Mummy Mountain

Hike: Mummy Mountain (Mummy's Tummy) — up and back or closed loop
Trailhead: North Loop (Deer Creek) — marked
Distance: 11 miles — round trip
Elevation gain: 3,142 feet
Elevation peak: 11,542 feet
Time: 7 to 9 hours
Difficulty: 5
Danger level: 4
How easy to follow: 4
Children: no
Map: Mt. Charleston Peak, NEV

Directions: Take US 95 to State Route 157. Turn left on 157 and turn right onto State Route 158. Travel five miles to the North Loop trailhead sign located on the left (west) side of the road. (See Photo 1 in the Mummy Springs hike, p. 59.)

Overview: Hike the North Loop **trail** to Mummy Springs. From there, it's a **route** to the ridgeline, then another route to the chute that leads to the peak.

Comments: This hike will challenge you. Mummy Mountain is the second highest peak in Mt. Charleston.

The Hike: The trail starts off at an easy grade, wandering by ponderosa and pinion pine and mountain mahogany. June through September, a number of colorful flowers grow alongside the trail. To the east on Angel Peak rests a large, white, ball-shaped observatory, a good landmark to look for when descending. The trail meanders up a few moderate switchbacks before reaching a plateau; look NE for a good view. Several bristlecone pines scattered throughout this area indicate you're above 9,000 feet.

After 12 moderately steep switchbacks, the trail climbs to an elevation of 10,200 feet. It then descends 150 feet over the next third of a mile to Raintree, a 3,000-year-old bristlecone pine. A wooden sign next to Raintree indicates options and distances. Go right and follow the trail a third of a mile to Mummy Springs.

At Mummy Springs follow the path that veers to the left. Climb the steep path using the rock to pull yourself up. Once at the top of the waterfall, follow the path that travels along the left side of the spring. When you reach a small cliff, look for the class II chute in Photo 1 that takes you to the top of Mummy Springs.

Now for the hard part—you begin your ascent to the base of Mummy Mountain. If you have a compass, head up the mountain at 262 degrees. Without a compass, stand facing the ridgeline and head at an angle which approximates one o'clock. The direction is west. There's a path here, but it's hard to follow; people who hike this route have wandered on and off the path, obscuring it. This is a very steep class I trek. After a while, you'll notice a ridgeline to your right. Stay parallel to it and go between the two outcrops that come into view as you get near the top. At the top, you'll be between Mummy's Toe and Tummy (Mummy Mountain). If you can't see the jagged pinnacles, you're too far to the left. Walk NW along the ridgeline until

Photo 1

you see them. Mummy's Tummy lies NW (right) of where you stand. Walk to the very top of the ridgeline and enjoy the magnificent view. You can see part of the North Loop Trail winding through the mountains. To the SSE is Griffith Peak, and to the SW lies Charleston Peak. To your right are the jagged pinnacles. These are not only extremely dangerous to climb, but they don't get you any closer to Mummy's Tummy.

From this spot you hike westerly in front of the outcrops and behind the jagged pinnacles. From your current viewpoint it looks like you'll be walking off a cliff side; don't worry. Look for the tree in Photo 2. When you get to the tree (less than 100 yards), you'll see a faint path to the left that winds against the backside of the pinnacles. It's an easy climb down to the path.

Now you traverse the east base of Mummy Mountain in a NW direction until you reach the correct chute that goes up to Mummy's Tummy, the main part of Mummy Mountain. The traverse is less than a mile. The path hugs the base at first, then descends about 75 yards to follow a smaller set of cliffs (8-10 feet). The path comes to a huge bristlecone pine that has fallen upward onto the path. Most of the time, there's a path to follow. When the path splits, stay on the lower fork and look for a large rock the path descends around. Photo 3 is an overview of this traverse.

Photo 2

Photo 3

You'll come to a false chute, but continue along the path for another four to eight minutes until you see the correct chute in Photo 4. Climb up on the left side of this chute to avoid the talus. Three quarters of the way up the chute, traverse to the smaller chute. (See Photos 5 and 6.) This traverse is steep and filled with talus—be careful. A dead tree that leans at a 45 degree angle marks the beginning of Susan's Chute, which takes you up to the landing. It's a class III climb to the landing. (See Photo 6 for a close-up of Susan's Chute.) Once on the landing, go around to the left (north) along the base of the wall to the steep walk-up to the summit of Mummy Mountain. The

Photo 4

The Landing

Photo 5

walk-up is easier if you stay on the left side and hike on the solid rock.

Congratulations, you made it! At the top, a cairn with a sign-in book sits at the highest point off to the SE. A three-foot-high log shelter lies about 60 yards to the west of the sign-in book. This is a perfect place to escape the wind and have lunch. To the SW lies Charleston Peak; to the SE lies Griffith Peak and Red Rock Canyon; a little farther to the east is Las Vegas.

To Descend: You have two options: retrace your steps, or make a partial loop out of the hike by hiking down the west side of Mummy Mountain to the North Loop Trail. Start by walking to the west of the shelter and descending the class II chute. Descend the right (north) side of the chute. At the bottom of the chute go left onto the path and follow it as it heads south, paralleling Mummy Mountain until it turns SW toward the North Rim ridgeline. Once at the North Rim ridgeline, the

Dead Tree

Photo 6

path heads west and descends about 100 yards down the north (right) side of the ridgeline. This is where people lose the path.

All you have to do is follow the path down to where it goes across a rocky bluff. Climb down the far side of the rocky bluff (class I or II). The path resumes westerly along the North Rim ridgeline and is easy to follow. At the dead log, the path forks to the south (left) and heads down the scree to intersect the North Loop Trail. This is an extremely steep descent; be careful on the scree. You'll have no problem spotting the North Loop Trail. Go east (left) and follow it back to Raintree, about a mile and a half. From Raintree hike back to the trailhead. This alternate route is recommended if you're tired or enjoy hiking back a different way.

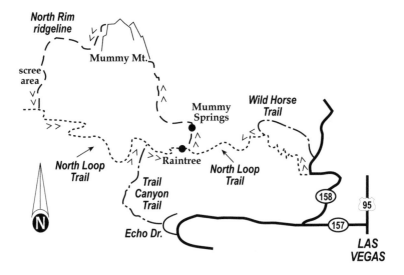

♦ ♦ ♦

North Loop to Charleston Peak

Hike: North Loop to Charleston Peak — up and back
or open loop
Trailhead: junction of North Loop and Trail Canyon
Distance: 8 to 10 miles — one way
Elevation gain: Trail Canyon 4,213 ft.; Deer Creek 3,554 ft.
Elevation peak: 11,918 feet
Time: all day
Difficulty: 5
Danger level: 3
How easy to follow: 1
Children: no
Map: Charleston Peak, NEV

Directions: The trailhead is at the junction of Trail Canyon
and North Loop Trail (Deer Creek). It's a two-mile hike from
the Trail Canyon Trail or a four-mile hike from North Loop
Trail to this junction. See Trail Canyon (p. 34) for its trailhead
location.

Overview: The **trail** starts in a northerly direction climbing to
the North Ridge Rim, then heads southerly to the base of Mt.
Charleston. A killer one-mile trek puts you at the highest point
in southern Nevada.

Comments: If you want to feel like you're on top of the world,
this is the hike. The area's only treeless peak engenders the
feeling of standing at the top of a mountain that's a lot higher

than it really is. You must come prepared for this all-day hike. The reason for beginning the description of this hike at the junction is to give you the option of starting the hike at either of the two trailheads.

The Hike: From the junction of Trail Canyon and North Loop trails, the trail heads NW around Mummy Mountain. The grade is moderate as you enter the dead forest, where a "people-caused fire" in the late 1940s burned more than 500 acres. Scattered throughout the dead forest are aspens that turn orange and yellow in the fall. By looking to the left (south), you'll get a great view of Kyle Canyon; directly ahead looms Charleston Peak.

About a mile and a half from the junction is Cave Springs. Water runs into a horse trough and a path goes up to a cave-like overhang above the horse trough. The North Loop Trail continues southerly through the dead forest and aspens as the grade becomes moderate. It makes a horseshoe bend and heads NE before switching back and heading west toward the North Rim Ridge. A little less than a mile from the horseshoe bend, a series of bluffs to the left of the trail offers great views of Kyle Canyon. The aspens disappear up here, since the elevation is more than 10,000 feet.

The trail flattens out as it heads SW around the series of bluffs. The North Rim Ridge is only a few hundred feet above the trail. Charleston Peak comes in and out of view as the trail starts to imitate a roller coaster. The trail flattens out again and cuts through a forest of bristlecone pines. Three overlooks to the north offer the first views of the Sisters, Mack's Peak, and McFarland Peak. The third overlook also has a great view of Charleston Peak and Kyle Canyon, making this one of the best views in the Mt. Charleston Area. The trail continues in a SW direction as it winds along the base of cliffs. A few short but steep switchbacks bring the trail up to the North Rim Ridge. As the final switchback turns to the left, a short path to the right leads to the ridge. Plan on spending a few minutes catching your breath while you take in the fantastic view of all the northern mountains of the Mt. Charleston Area. (See Photo 1.)

As the trail heads south toward Charleston Peak, look to

Mc Farland Peak   Mack's Peak   Sisters

Photo 1

the left (east) for great views of Kyle Canyon. The trail remains flat as it heads SE below Devil's Thumb. (See Photo 2.) Mt. Charleston comes in and out of view as the trail traverses the rocky ledges. Look for fossils in the rocks, left over from when this area was once an ancient sea. Trees are scarce since the elevation is more than 11,000 feet. The trail heads around a few bluffs; it seems to take forever to arrive at the base of Charleston Peak. It makes one switchback and climbs around a final bluff before the mile-long hike to the peak.

Charleston Peak   Devil's Thumb

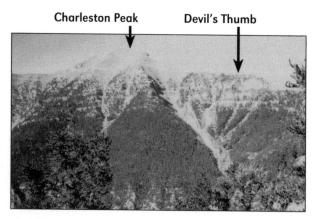

Photo 2

The last mile is a series of steep switchbacks. The grade is 17%. The peak is always in sight, since there are no trees to block your view. It's important to drink plenty of water before and during this final mile. One cause of altitude sickness is a lack of water.

Congratulations, you are standing at the highest point in southern Nevada. (See the South Loop Trail description for more about the top of the peak.)

If you parked your car at Trail Canyon trailhead, hiked up to the peak on the North Loop Trail, and are hiking down the South Loop Trail, there's a shortcut to your car. Walk out of Cathedral Rock Picnic Area and go past the parking lot and stairs. To your left begins a trail wide enough for a car. Follow the trail to its trailhead, which is on Echo Drive. Turn left onto Echo Drive and walk past the turnoff for Mary Jane Falls to Trail Canyon trailhead. This shortens the walk between the trailheads by a half mile.

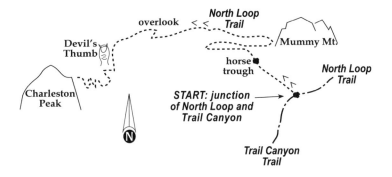

♦ ♦ ♦

South Sister

Hike: South Sister — up and back
Trailhead: End of Mack's Canyon Road
Distance: 6 miles — round trip
Elevation gain: 1,482 feet
Elevation peak: 10,175 feet
Time: 4 to 5 hours
Difficulty: 3
Danger level: 3
How easy to follow: 4
Children: no
Map: Charleston Peak, NEV

Directions: Take US 95 to State Route 156. Go left on 156; turn right onto Mack's Canyon Road. If you pass the intersection of 158/156, you've gone too far. Follow the gravel road till it dead-ends (4.3 miles). A four-wheel drive is not needed.

Overview: The **route** follows a spring and climbs to a ridgeline, then crosses the ridgeline for the final scramble to the peak.

Comments: The Sisters are twin peaks about a half mile apart. Great views of Lee Canyon, Mack's Peak, and McFarland Peak can be seen from the South Sister. It's very steep and narrow at the peak.

The Hike: The unmarked trail begins by the large boulders that block cars from continuing on the gravel road. The grade is easy as the gravel road heads south. Soon the South Sister comes into view on the left. The gravel road turns into a path as it crosses an unnamed spring several times. Water flows year round in the spring. The incline increases, as does lush greenery in the area. The path goes up a steep incline and intersects another path. Go right onto this new path for about 50 yards until it disappears and the hike turns into a cross-country route. From this point head

Photo 1

north up the mountain to gain a ridgeline. This is a very steep trek; it's best to zigzag up the mountain.

Once on the ridgeline look SE to see the South Sister you'll soon be standing on. A path begins on the ridgeline as it heads toward the peak. The incline is mostly moderate with only a few steep sections. Once at the summit, the ridgeline flattens out and offers great views of Charleston Peak, the North Sister, McFarland Peak, and Mack's Peak. The road below to the south

Photo 2

Photo 3

is Old Mill Road. The South Sister lies 60 degrees to the NE. (See Photo 1.)

The route crosses a saddle before making the final climb to the base of the South Sister. A faint path leads to the base. This is the hardest part of the hike. (See the white line in Photo 2 for an overview of the route.) At the saddle go left into the chute that goes up to the peak. (See Photo 3.) At the top of the chute go left again and scramble to the peak. A sign-in book in a cairn marks the peak. It is very narrow along the peak—be careful. The peak extends for about 75 yards before dropping straight down 50 feet.

To Descend: Retrace your steps.

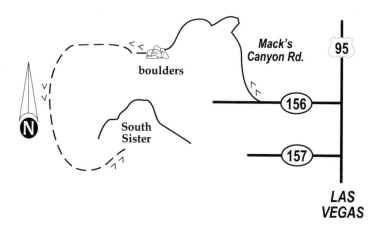

♦ ♦ ♦

Mack's Peak

Hike: Mack's Peak — up and back
Trailhead: End of Mack's Canyon Road
Distance: 6 miles — round trip
Elevation gain: 1,177 feet
Elevation peak: 10,033 feet
Time: 5 hours
Difficulty: 4
Danger level: 4
How easy to follow: 4
Children: no
Map: Charleston Peak, NEV

Directions: Take US 95 to State Route 156. Go left on 156; turn right at the Mack's Canyon sign. If you reach the intersection of 158/156, you've gone too far. Follow the gravel road till it deadends (4.3 miles). A four-wheel drive is not needed.

Overview: The **route** begins along a gravel road, then runs up a dry wash to a saddle. Hike up the ridgeline to the base of Mack's Peak. Traverse the base to the chute that leads you to the top.

Comments: Mack's Peak is a tough mountain, requiring plenty of rock scrambling. The knife-edged peak enhances the feeling of standing on the summit of a mountain. This hike is not recommended for people scared of heights, since the peak is highly exposed.

The Hike: The unmarked route begins where boulders block vehicles from continuing on the gravel road; Mack's Peak is not visible from the trailhead due to the ridgeline that the route eventually climbs. The route starts off heading SSW (210 degrees) and is a continuation of the gravel road. This part of the hike has a gentle incline as it passes white fir and pinion pine. About 200 yards from the trailhead, go right (west) into a dry creekbed, using the tree stump in Photo 1 as your landmark. About 100 yards up the creekbed a huge tree has fallen into the creekbed. Pass it to the right. Just after the tree the creekbed divides, take the left fork. The route becomes steep as the creekbed climbs toward the ridgeline.

Once the creekbed disappears, head WNW (296 degrees) toward Mack's Peak, which can be seen from this point. The mountain to the left is McFarland Peak. Aim for the saddle. If you go too far to the right (east), you'll be climbing up a ridge, only to have to hike down the west side of the same ridge. The closer you get to the saddle, the easier it is to adjust your course. Near the top of the saddle bristlecone pines are abundant.

Once at the saddle, stay on the ridgeline and head west toward Mack's Peak. The trek to the base is steep. Photo 2 shows the direction of travel. Cairns and red tape mark a path

Stump

Photo 1

Photo 2

leading to the base of Mack's Peak. At the base the path traverses north along the cliffs. When the cliffs pull away, the path goes straight up toward the base. This a short but very steep trek. The path again heads north. In about 50 yards the path runs into the chute that leads to the peak.

A large burnt bristlecone pine and red tape mark the chute. (See Photo 3.) There are lots of loose rocks and gravel in the chute. It's best to veer to the right side, staying on limestone ledges, which avoids much of the loose rock. At the top of the chute go right, making an almost 180-degree turn, and follow the path to the peak. It's about 75 yards from the top of the chute to the peak.

At the peak a cairn contains a sign-in book. The peak extends northerly and becomes very narrow past the sign-in book. A second peak lies 200 yards to the north; however, it's very tricky coming off the north side of the first peak. Massive McFarland Peak lies to the SW and the Sisters rest to the SE.

To Descend: Go east of the sign-in book and look for red tape marking the descent. This is the same route as the way up, but it is easy to become disorientated at the peak. When the route appears to deadend, go left into the chute. If a group is descending the chute, individuals should descend one at a time, then walk to the far right (out of the line of fire) before the next person starts down. Most people descend the lower part of the chute by sliding down the rocks. The rocks tumble off the ledge and crash down by the entrance of the chute.

Photo 3

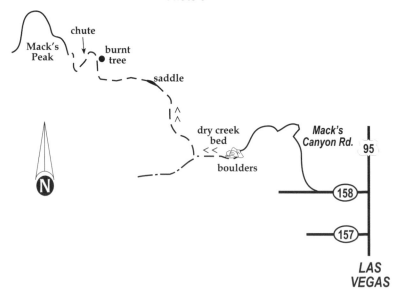

♦ ♦ ♦

Bristlecone Trail

Hike: Bristlecone Trail — closed loop
Trailhead: Upper parking lot at Las Vegas Ski and Snowboard Resort
Distance: 5 miles
Elevation gain: 600 feet
Elevation peak: no peak
Time: 2.5 to 3.5 hours
Difficulty: 1
Danger Level: 1
How easy to follow: 1
Children: yes
Map: Charleston Peak, NEV

Directions: Take US 95 north to State Route 156. Go left (west) on 156 until it ends at Las Vegas Ski and Snowboard Resort and park at the far (west) end of the parking lot. The unmarked trailhead is on the west side at the upper end of the parking lot. (See Photo 1.)

Overview: The **trail** makes a giant loop to the north of the ski area.

Comments: This is the most hiked trail in the area. It's a perfect trail for introducing children to hiking. If you hike the entire loop, the end of the trail is about a half mile down the highway from the trailhead. Mountain bikes are allowed on the trail.

The Hike: The well-maintained trail starts off at an easy pace heading west, then forks. Take either fork, since the two trails come together again in about 100 yards. It winds through a thick forest of aspen and white fir that turn golden yellow in the fall. The trail ascends a series of switchbacks, while the trees help keep you cool during the moderate incline. After climbing to a summit, the trail snakes down the backside of a mountain. After two miles, the trail follows an abandoned gravel road. Soon

Photo 1

the trail forks again; the trail to the left goes to Bonanza Peak trailhead. Bonanza Trail is a 15-mile trail that passes Clark Pond, McFarland Peak, and Bonanza Peak.

The Bristlecone Trail follows the abandoned road and descends into a canyon. At about four miles, the trail passes the Old Mill Road. The Bristlecone Trail heads downhill to the right of a picnic area and terminates at a dirt parking lot. Follow the dirt road to 156. Walk west on 156 to the trailhead.

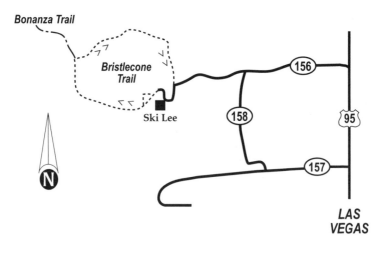

♦ ♦ ♦

Bonanza Trail

Hike: Bonanza Trail — open loop
Trailhead: Ski Lee — not marked
                 Cold Creek — marked
Distance: 15.3 miles — one way
Elevation gain: 2,300 feet
Elevation peak: no peak
Time: all day
Difficulty: 5
Danger level: 1
How easy to follow: 1
Children: no
Map: Charleston Peak, NEV and Willow Peak, NEV

Directions: Take US 95 to State Route 156. Go left (west) on 156 until it ends at Las Vegas Ski and Snowboard Resort and park at the far (west) end of the upper parking lot. The un-marked trailhead is on the west side of the parking lot. (See Photo 1 in the Bristlecone hike, previous page.)

Overview: The **trail** climbs several summits as it passes to the west of the Sisters and Mack's Peak, to the east of Clark Pond, and to the south of McFarland Peak. It passes beneath Bonanza Peak before descending to Bonanza Peak trailhead.

Comments: This hike takes you to some of the most remote areas in Mt. Charleston. The best way to approach this hike is with two groups of people. One group starts at Las Vegas Ski and Snowboard Resort trailhead; the other group starts at Bo-nanza Peak trailhead. When the groups meet, they exchange car keys. This avoids the car shuttle, which is a 45-minute drive.

The stronger group should start at Bonanza Peak trailhead.

The Hike: The first two miles of the hike are along the Bristlecone Trail. (See the Bristlecone hike, p. 79, for a description.) A sign stands at the intersection of Bristlecone Trail and the beginning of the Bonanza Trail. Go left onto Bonanza Trail. The trail starts at an easy pace, then turns into moderate switchbacks as it climbs to a saddle. At the saddle a path forks off to the left. It's a little less than a mile from the start of Bonanza Trail to the saddle. The trail climbs a series of steps up to a ridgeline; you're heading NW at this point. Once you reach the ridgeline, the trail stays to the west side of the mountain. One of the rugged-looking Sisters stands to your right. The backside of Mt. Charleston is seen by looking SSE. From this angle Mt. Charleston looks impossible to climb.

The trail becomes steep as it passes rock outcroppings and climbs to another ridgeline. At this ridgeline look for a 30-foot-high rock pinnacle as a reference point. It will be to your right. When the trail moves to the west side of the mountain, there's a good view of Clark Pond down and to the west. From this viewpoint, the water looks very green. The tough-looking mountain to the east (right) is Mack's Peak. The grade is easy along this section. As the trail heads west, it comes off the ridgeline and goes through an area with few trees. McFarland Peak lies directly ahead.

The trail climbs to another ridgeline and stays to the east as it makes its way to McFarland, then heads to the south as it goes around this giant mountain. From here, you start downhill on a series of short switchbacks. Right before the start of the switchbacks, look for a rock outcropping with a dead tree leaning against it. A faint path starts from here and leads to McFarland Peak. For a description of that hike see the McFarland hike on p. 84.

The trail continues west around McFarland and crosses a spring. About a half mile after crossing the spring, it turns northerly and the grade is mostly flat. In about two miles the trail crosses another spring: you're now past the halfway point. Soon after crossing the spring, the trail starts to climb the south side of Bonanza Mountain. It parallels Wood Springs before climbing a series of steep switchbacks just below Bonanza Peak. Up here the hiking is easy as the trail stays to the west of the ridgeline. It soon descends gently to a saddle. The saddle marks 11 miles in. From the saddle the trail descends switchbacks the last four miles down the NE side of Bonanza Mountain. The trail ends at the Bonanza trailhead.

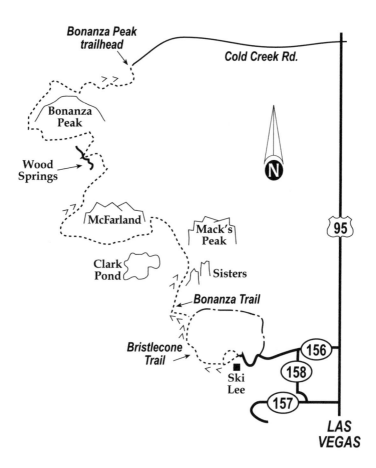

♦ ♦ ♦

McFarland Peak

Hike: McFarland Peak — up and back
Trailhead: Bristlecone Trail — Lee Canyon Ski Area
Distance: 13 miles — round trip
Elevation gain: 2,225 feet
Elevation peak: 10,742 feet
Time: 9 to 12 hours
Difficulty: 5
Danger level: 3
How easy to follow: 5
Children: no
Map: Charleston Peak, NEV

Directions: Take US 95 to State Route 156. Turn left onto 156 and follow it to the upper parking lot at Lee Canyon Ski Area. The unmarked Bristlecone trailhead begins at the NW corner of the parking lot. (See Photo 1 in the Bristlecone Trail hike, p. 80.)

Overview: It's a five-mile approach **trail,** then a **route** up the NW gully to a saddle. From the saddle it's an easy quarter mile to the peak.

Comments: If you want to test yourself, this is the hike. The five-mile approach trail is no piece of cake and the 1,000-foot scramble to the peak is a killer. Be careful of loose rocks. The idea is to follow a drainage up to a massive rock formation. At this formation a definite route is taken to reach the saddle.

The Hike: The first two miles of the hike follow the Bristle-cone Trail. A sign stands at the intersection of Bristlecone Trail and the start of Bonanza Trail. Go left to pick up the Bonanza Trail. The pace starts out easy, then turns into moderate switchbacks as it climbs to a saddle a little less than a mile from the start of Bonanza Trail. At the saddle, a path forks off to the left and the trail climbs a series of steps to a ridgeline. Once you reach the ridgeline, the trail stays to the west side of the mountain. One of the Sisters can been seen on the right.

The trail becomes steep as it passes by rock outcroppings and climbs to another ridgeline. (A rock pinnacle sits about 30 feet to the right.) Once the trail travels to the west side of the mountain, you get a view of Clark Pond by facing west and looking down into the valley. The rugged mountain to the right is Mack's Peak. As the trail heads west, it comes off the ridgeline and goes through an area with few trees. McFarland Peak lies directly ahead. The trail climbs to another ridgeline and then stays to the east of it as it makes its way to McFarland. Near McFarland, the trail heads south as it skirts the mountain.

At the beginning of this series of switchbacks, leave the trail and head toward the rock outcropping in Photo 1. To the right of the rock outcropping a faint path heads north (10 degrees) toward a small rock wall. The path crosses over two fallen trees before reaching the wall. Near the wall, head to-

Photo 1

ward the drainage that lies about 100 yards west. The drainage is easily navigated, with little chance of dislodging rocks. Scramble up the drainage the best you can. At the end of the drainage, head a few hundred yards toward the massive rock formation in Photo 2. You might see an orange ribbon tied to a tree; make sure you are to the west (left) of the tree. The route goes about 50 feet east of the west wall and passes a small cave. Stay to the right of the next rock outcropping. The ground changes from dirt to rock as you head toward the massive rock formation.

Photo 2

Once at the rock formation, stay to the right of it to start the climb. Go between the rock and the tree in Photo 3. Cross over a large fallen log and hike along the north side of the same rock formation. (See Photo 4.) Once past the massive rock formation, head north up the mountain and look for the large fallen tree in Photo 5. A rock cairn sits in a fork of the tree. From this point a pine-needle path weaves between rocks and trees. (See Photo 6 for the start of this path.) Photo 7 looks down from the top of this path, where you'll find the tree in Photo 8. Go between the tree and the rock wall; climb up the wall and follow the path to a gap. A large bristlecone pine is on the right side and a half-

Photo 3

Photo 4

dead bristlecone pine sits on the left side of the gap. A rock cairn might lie by the half-dead bristlecone pine.

Once past the gap, traverse the scree toward the west wall. (See Photo 9.) At the west wall a path starts, passes a large cave, then heads toward the saddle. Once at the saddle, head east (right) and follow the ridgeline for a quarter mile to the peak. This part of the trek is easy, and the views get progressively better. A small cairn with a sign-in book marks the peak. You'll find excellent views of Charleston Peak, Mack's Peak, Bonanza Peak, and Mummy Mountain waiting for you at the peak. Few people have made it to the top of this mountain. Take pride in your accomplishment.

To Descend: Retrace your steps.

Photo 5

Photo 6

Photo 7

Photo 8

Photo 9

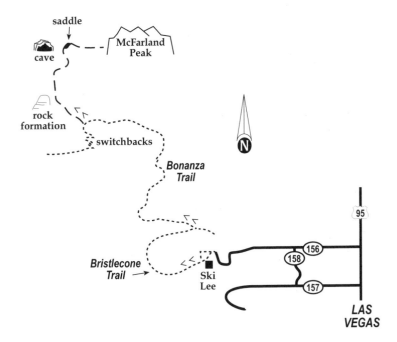

◆ ◆ ◆

Bonanza Peak

Hike: Bonanza Peak — up and back
Trailhead: Cold Creek Trailhead — marked
Distance: 10 miles — round trip
Elevation gain: 2,300 feet
Elevation peak: 10,400 feet
Time: 5 to 6 hours
Difficulty: 3
Danger level: 1
How easy to follow: 1
Children: no
Map: Charleston Peak, NEV and Willow Peak, NEV

Directions: From Las Vegas take US 95 nineteen miles past the turnoff for State Route 157 to Cold Creek Road. Turn left (west) onto the unmarked Cold Creek Road and travel 16 miles until the road deadends into the Cold Creek trailhead. (See Photo 1.) The last two miles is a gravel road. A four-wheel drive is not needed. Note: Cold Creek Road is not on Nevada maps.

Overview: The **trail** is a series of switchbacks that climbs to a saddle. From the saddle, the trail heads south to the peak.

Comments: Though Bonanza Peak is part of the SMNRA, many locals do not consider it part of the Mt. Charleston Area, because it's past State Route 156. But the drive is only a few minutes longer than to Lee Canyon Ski Area, and the opportunity for solitude and catching a glimpse of wild horses roaming free makes the few extra miles worth the effort.

The Hike: The well-maintained trail starts off at a leisurely pace with a slight incline. (See Photo 1 for the sign at the trailhead and Photo 2 for a view of Bonanza Peak from the trailhead.) The trail ascends a series of switchbacks as it winds through the ponderosa pines. The grade becomes steeper dur-

ing the switchbacks, but the view eases the pain. By looking to the SW, you can see the backside of Mummy Mountain.

You can't help but notice the acres of burned trees from a fire years ago. This serves as a reminder just how dry conditions become in these mountains. The trail becomes steeper as it switches back among the white firs. In this area, many white lupin and bluish phalux flowers grow alongside the trail. After numerous switchbacks, the trail heads in a SE direction and flattens out. Looking up toward the ridgeline you'll see a rocky cliff.

Photo 1

Once at the saddle, take a break and keep your eyes open for wild horses grazing. Judging from the amount of horse manure scattered in this area, this seems to be one of their favor-

Bonanza Peak

Photo 2

ite places. By looking west you can see the town of Pahrump. A hard-to-follow trail starts at the saddle and heads north toward the Natural Arch rock formation and ends at Willow Peak, which is three miles from the saddle. This is a long, tough hike with plenty of rock scrambling (see the Willow Peak hike, p. 94).

From the saddle, the Bonanza Peak Trail heads in a SW direction staying below the ridgeline to the east. After a short incline, the trail flattens out into the most enjoyable part of the hike. Pine cones litter the trail, as you hike among the bristlecone pines. A large rock outcrop indicates the peak is close. As the trail comes near the ridgeline, you can make a short cross-country trek up to the ridgeline. Once at the ridgeline, head SE (right) till you see a large cairn. The cairn marks the peak and contains a sign-in log found in a plastic jar. An alternative to the cross-country trek is to stay on the main trail and watch carefully for a path off to the left that heads toward the peak. This side path is easily missed. Bonanza Peak is not as prominent as some of the other peaks covered in this book. Scrambling up to the ridgeline and following it till you reach the peak is the surest way of finding it.

The view from Bonanza Peak is both unique and surprising. The uniqueness comes from seeing the various peaks in Mt. Charleston from this angle, and the surprise is how close you are to them. To the SE (140 degrees) is Charleston Peak. From this angle, it looks unapproachable. Mack's Peak lies almost due east at 80 degrees. It is the closest peak and appears to be only a couple of miles away. The rugged-looking McFarland Peak lies to the SW of Mack's Peak.

Another hike starting from this same trailhead is the Bonanza Trail to the parking lot of the Las Vegas Ski and Snowboard Resort. Instead of turning off the trail to go to Bonanza Peak, continue for 10.3 miles on the trail to the ski resort. The entire trail is 15.3 miles. A car shuttle is a must, since the beginning and ending points are 30 miles apart (by road).

To Descend: Retrace your steps.

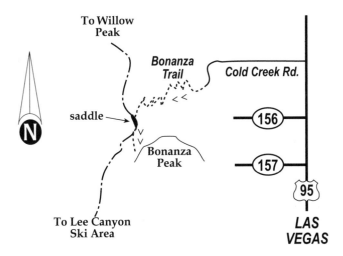

◆ ◆ ◆

Willow Peak

Hike: Willow Peak — up and back
Trailhead: Bonanza Trail — marked
Distance: 16 miles — round trip
Elevation gain: 1,864 feet
Elevation peak: 9,964 feet
Time: 8-10 hours
Difficulty: 4
Danger level: 2
How easy to follow: 5
Children: no
Map: Charleston Peak, NEV and Willow Peak, NEV

Directions: Take US 95 to Cold Creek Road (19 miles past the turnoff for State Route 157), turn left, and travel 16 miles until the road deadends into the Bonanza trailhead. The last 2.1 miles of the 16 miles is a gravel road. A four-wheel-drive is not needed. Note: Cold Creek Road is not on Nevada maps.

Overview: The **trail** climbs to a ridgeline, then it becomes a **route** to the peak.

Comments: This hike offers a chance to use your navigational skills, since part of it is a route. The peak is in sight most of the time, making it an easy landmark. There's no correct route, but the one suggested here makes the trek the shortest and easiest.

The Hike: The well-maintained Bonanza Trail starts off at a leisurely pace with a slight incline. The trail winds on a series of switchbacks as it passes by ponderosa pines. The grade becomes steep during the switchbacks, but the pain is offset by the better view.

You can't help noticing the acres of burned trees left from a fire years ago. They serve as a reminder as to just how dry conditions become in these mountains. The trail turns steeper as it switches back among the white fir. In this area many white lupine and bluish phalux grow alongside the trail. After numerous switchbacks, the trail heads SE and flattens out. Look up toward the ridgeline to see a rocky cliff. Once at the saddle, head west (290 degrees), leaving the Bonanza Trail, and follow the path up through the rock outcropping seen in Photo 1.

The path, which disappears at times, hugs the ridgeline, climbing up and over rock outcroppings. When the path disappears at an outcrop with a 10-foot section of rock that lies between scrub oak, climb up between the bushes. You can avoid the next outcrop by going to the right (east) on the path. Look for a half-burnt bristlecone pine at the next outcrop marking the way up. The route flattens out temporarily before the next outcrop. Look for a low point to climb up and over. The path appears again, making it easy to follow the route. If you're on the correct route you'll pass a dead bristlecone, 20-25 feet long, leaning against an outcrop. The path goes left (west) around the next outcrop. From this point you can see Willow Peak by looking NW (298 degrees).

Photo 1

The path keeps to the left (west) of the next outcroppings and is generally flat. Follow the path to avoid climbing over the rocks. When the route comes to a saddle, look right (east) to see the burnt forest that covers the east side of the mountain. Pick up the gravel and pine-needle trail that lies about 20 feet to the right (west) of the outcrop. Less than a half mile from the saddle is a natural arch, a great place to take pictures. (See Photo 2.)

From the Arch, the path becomes easier to follow as it

traverses, and then hugs, the west side of the ridgeline. The path crosses a talus and scree area before hugging the west side of the next outcrop, then descends to go around another obstacle. Willow Peak is in view at this point. The path is 75 to 100 feet below the ridgeline as it traverses another scree area. The path be-

Photo 2

comes hard to follow, but keep heading toward Willow Peak. (See Photo 3.) Shortly past the outcrop the path disappears. From here you want to gain the ridgeline. Head east (60 to 70 degrees) to the bottom set of cliffs that make up the ridgeline. Once at the cliffs, look for the chute in Photo 4. Climb up the

chute and stay on the ridgeline as much as possible. Occasionally you'll drop off the ridgeline to the SW. Eventually you come to an obvious saddle. Photo 5 shows the suggested route from the saddle to the peak.

When you come to the last bluff before the peak, go around to the left and look for the log in Photo 6. Climb up the rock face in Photo 6.

Peak

Photo 3

Once up, head toward the far side of the peak about a quarter of a mile away. A cairn with a sign-in book marks the peak.

To Descend: Retrace your steps.

Photo 4

Photo 5

Photo 6

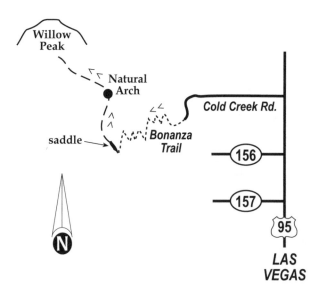

♦RED ROCK CANYON♦

Red Rock Canyon, a mere 20 miles from downtown Las Vegas, is the Bureau of Land Management's recreation show-case in southern Nevada. It's nearly 200,000 acres of multicol-ored sandstone, ancient limestone, canyons and mountains, washes and waterfalls, and a variety of flora and fauna. Most people who go to Red Rock don't hike. Instead, they drive around the Scenic Loop in their cars, photographing the breath-taking views.

Unlike many other popular hiking locales, most hikes in Red Rock Canyon are not crowded. You'll be lucky (or un-lucky, depending on your point of view) to see another per-son while hiking. Currently, permits are not required for day hikes.

The Visitors Center at Red Rock is open from 8:30 am to 4:30 pm daily; (702) 363-1921. The rangers are knowledgeable and happy to answer questions. Inside, you can avail yourself of bathrooms, water, and an interesting museum containing a fantastic model of the Red Rock area. I highly recommend that you study this visual reference before hiking. There are also books to buy and use for reference. Other than at the Visitors Center, handicap facilities and restrooms are located at Sand-stone Quarry, Willow Springs, and Pine Creek.

Camping will be available at the new campgrounds lo-cated about a mile before the turnoff to Red Rock Canyon on the south (left) side of State Route 159. Water, porta potties, fire pits, trash collection, and picnic tables will be furnished. Camping is also allowed above the 5,000-foot level, but you

FAST FACTS—RED ROCK CANYON

Location: 20 miles west of Las Vegas.
Directions: Drive west on Charleston Blvd. (State Route 159) and follow the signs. Turn right into Red Rock.
Visitor Center: 8:30 to 4:30 daily year-round, (702) 363-1921.
Scenic Loop: The 13-mile, one-way, paved road that circles the canyon is open 7 am to dusk.
Fees: $5 per car or $20 for a yearly pass.
Permits: None for day hiking.
Camping: New campground (when opened, about a mile east of the park entrance) and areas above 5,000 feet—permits required.
Fires: Ground fires and wood gathering prohibited.
Best time to hike: October through May.
Hikes: Less than a mile to 15+ miles. All difficulties.
Managed by: BLM, (702) 647-5000.
Size: 195,610 acres.
Elevation range: 3,394 feet to 7,092 feet.
Bicycles: Only on the Rocky Gap Road and Scenic Loop.
Mountain bikes: Only on the Rocky Gap Road and Scenic Loop.
Horses: Yes—limited trails.
Dogs: Yes—designated trails on a leash. Do not take on scrambling routes.
Runners: Yes.
Gasoline: Not available.
Firearms: Not permitted.
Collecting: No artifacts, fossils or plant materials may be collected within the boundaries of Red Rock Canyon.

need to obtain a permit in advance at the Visitors Center. The permits are good for two days. Leave the permit in the glove compartment of your car. A $5 entrance fee per car is charged; you can also to purchase a yearly pass for $20.

Most of the trailheads are accessed via the Scenic Loop.

All mileage figures to the trailheads start from the Scenic Loop gate. As I write this, a new entrance road to Red Rock is being built. I've been told that the Scenic Loop gate will remain at the same location. But because of the new access road, there's a two-tenths-of-a-mile discrepancy between the mileage cited in the book and the mile markers on the Scenic Loop. It's nothing to worry about; all of the parking areas and pullouts are well-marked. The Scenic Loop gates are open from 7 am to dusk. You should plan to finish your hike before dark. Hiking after dark can be very dangerous and isn't recommended.

The Canyons

All five canyons covered in this book are located in Red Rock. All can be accessed via the Scenic Loop, with the exception of First Creek, which is accessed by State Route 159. The canyons are: Ice Box, Pine Creek, Juniper, Oak Creek, and First Creek. Hiking through the washes in the canyons offers some of the most scenic sights in Red Rock. Water cascading down multicolored sandstone, bighorn sheep running up near-vertical canyon walls, and sunlight dancing through the canyons all contribute to a unique hiking experience that will not be soon forgotten.

All of the canyon hikes require some bouldering, which involves climbing up, over, and down boulders. Most hikers find bouldering one of the most enjoyable forms of hiking. One secret of bouldering is to try to maintain a constant level, instead of climbing up and down each boulder. Good hikers hop from boulder to boulder as much as possible. This quickens the pace and saves wear and tear on knee joints.

Each canyon has at least one short hike to a pool, waterfall (maybe dry), or other interesting stopping point. These hikes accommodate beginners and families. Serious hikers and people in top shape can follow the canyons to various peaks. Hiking up Juniper Canyon leads to Juniper Peak; hiking through Oak Creek leads to Rainbow Wall; and Mt. Wilson Peak can be reached by hiking through First Creek. These are long tough hikes that include sections of class III climbing. They should be attempted only by experienced hikers.

I haven't given step-by-step accounts of hiking in the canyons. This would be impossible and take the fun out of the bouldering. I identify the correct forks to travel and suggest ways around some of the major obstacles. You might find better ways around the obstacles than those that I've suggested, possibly due to the amount of water you encounter in the creekbeds and the water temperature. Normally, you can climb over the boulders or take a path around them—some are as large as small rooms!

I have supplied less description on how to get past the obstacles on the difficult canyon hikes, since only experienced hikers should attempt them. I offer ways around the few obstacles in the washes on the shorter hikes to make them options for beginners and families.

All of the canyon hikes start out on established trails that lead to the canyon. Unfortunately, most of the trails end before entering the washes. The trails often deteriorate into dozens of paths that enter the wash at different points. It's impossible to supply exact descriptions on how to follow these paths. The trick is to pick the path that avoids the brush that lies between you and the wash. If you find a good path, be sure to note where it descends into the wash so you can find it on the way back. This makes the return hike much easier.

Finding and staying on the established trails and visible paths also makes good environmental sense. With dozens of paths spider-webbing off in all direction, it makes it impossible to follow the same route. This is not to say that you'll get lost, rather to point out that indiscriminately creating dozens of paths harms the environment and makes it harder for you, the hiker, to follow the established trails and paths. This also applies to cutting switchbacks in the Mt. Charleston Area.

It's virtually impossible to get lost in the canyons, since most of the time you can see the entrance. Simply turn around and follow the wash out of the canyon. Returning is quicker, since you'll now be able to climb down some of the obstacles you had to go around on the way up. And for whatever reason, it seems you always find an easier and quicker way back through the maze of paths that leads to the main trail.

If you're new to bouldering, I recommend that you start with the short hike into the south fork of Pine Creek. This hike is easy, goes to an interesting spot, and gives you a taste of bouldering through the canyons (see p. 194).

Bridge Mountain

The Bridge Mountain hike is one of the best hikes in this book; a hiker could spend a week exploring this huge sandstone mountain. From a hidden forest to 1,000-foot drops, Bridge offers a diversity of unique experiences for the hiker. From a distance, Bridge Mountain looks impossible to climb. It's only on closer inspection that impossible changes to, "I'll watch someone go first and think about it." Actually, it's not as difficult as it looks. If you've climbed Turtlehead Jr., you can climb Bridge.

Bridge Mountain sits between Pine Creek Canyon and Ice Box Canyon. These two canyons give Bridge its 1,000-foot dropoffs, and actually make it easy to stay on course. The trail to Bridge Mountain starts at Red Rock Summit, which is located on Rocky Gap Road. No longer maintained by the county, the old road to Pahrump has deteriorated to the point that even four-wheel-drive vehicles can get stuck. This nine-mile road connects Willow Springs parking area and Lovell Canyon Road. It's more than four miles from Lovell Canyon Road to Red Rock Summit and five miles from Willow Springs to Red Rock Summit. A four-wheel-drive vehicle can get farther up Rocky Gap Road from Lovell Canyon than from Willow Springs. If you don't have four-wheel drive, Willow Springs is a longer walk, but a shorter drive from Las Vegas. Either way, without a four-wheel drive it's a long walk to Red Rock Summit.

Bridge Mountain is an all-day affair and daylight is critical. It's too hot to hike Bridge during the longer summer days, so on the shorter fall days an early start is essential. Since Willow Springs is located on the Scenic Loop, you can't start before 7 a.m. You can, however, start anytime by accessing Rocky Gap Road via Lovell Canyon Road. Starting from Lovell Canyon Road is a shorter walk, but a longer drive and very desolate. You don't want car trouble out here—it's 10 miles to the nearest business. (See p. 176.)

Willow Springs

Willow Springs is located 7.3 miles past the Scenic Loop gate. A half-mile-long paved road leads to the parking lot. There are restrooms and picnic tables, but there's no drinkable water. Willow Springs is the starting point for many hikes, ranging from easy one-milers to all-day 15-plus-mile hikes.

Rocky Gap Road (also called Old Potato Road) begins at the end of the Willow Springs parking lot. This was the main road between Las Vegas and Pahrump years ago. Many of the longer hikes start at the beginning of Rocky Gap Road. A non-four-wheel-drive vehicle can travel about a half mile up the road before having to pull to the side and park. Four-wheel drives have traveled the entire road, but I don't recommend it.

To the north of the Willow Springs parking lot lies White Rock Hills Peak, to the west are the gray mountains of La Madre, and to the south are the major peaks that make up the Escarpment.

The Escarpment comprises, from north to south: North Peak, Bridge Mountain, Juniper Peak, Rainbow Peak, Mt. Wilson, and Indecision Peak. You can access Rainbow, Wilson, and Indecision from State Route 159. This eliminates restrictive starting and returning times, since the trailheads are not located on the Scenic Loop. Hikes to these peaks are all-day affairs and are best attempted during March and April when the days are longer, but the temperatures are still moderate. The North Peak/Bridge area is the Escarpment's most popular region for hikers.

Indecision Peak

Indecision Peak is the only peak along the Escarpment not accessed by a canyon. The grueling straight-up assault on the mountain's east face makes the lungs scream and the legs ache. And we call this fun! The approach is relatively free of brush compared to bouldering through First Creek. The views from the various overlooks of Bonnie Springs and Spring Mountain State Park are splendid.

The secondary limestone Indecision Peak lies to the west of the sandstone peak. It's a moderate mile-and-a-half walk; however, the views are not as dramatic as the sandstone peak.

I list the elevation of the sandstone peak from the Blue Diamond, NEV, topo map, but it's suspect. The limestone peak is listed as 1,044 feet higher than the sandstone peak (same topo map). I don't know if either elevation is correct, but to

Indecision Peak

maintain consistency I use the elevations from the topo maps. (See p. 239.)

DIFFICULTY INDEX

◆ ◆ ◆

Calico Hills I Overlook

Hike: Calico Hills I Overlook — up and back
Trailhead: Calico Hills I parking lot — marked
Distance: 2 miles — round trip
Elevation gain: 500 feet
Elevation peak: 4,300 feet
Time: 2 hours
Difficulty: 3
Danger level: 3
How easy to follow: 5
Children: no
Map: La Madre Mtn., NEV

Directions: The signed pulloff for Calico Hills I Overlook is located about one mile past the Scenic Loop gate.

Overview: The **route** goes across the wash, to a gully, and up the gully to the overlook.

Comments: This is a good hike to try out your scrambling skills. The overlook offers good views of Calico Basin and Las Vegas.

The Hike: Descend NE down the gravel trail onto the sandstone. Turn right, going between the sandstone boulders, and scramble down the sandstone slabs until you see the wash. Cross the wash and hike east diagonally up the sandstone ledges. (See Photo 1.) To the east a large boulder, "Ridgeline Rock," sits on the ridgeline. The trick is to head in the direction of Ridgeline Rock until you arrive at the correct chute. Photo 2 highlights Ridgeline Rock.

Climb down the slab and either leap onto "Jump Rock" and over to the next slab, or climb down and around Jump Rock. (See Photo 3.) Scramble up the slab and walk through the alleyway still heading toward Ridgeline Rock. Once past the bush in Photo 2, turn left and follow the dirt path until it deadends into the sandstone mound. Look for the chute that'll be to your right. (See Photo 4.) It's easiest to climb halfway up the chute and then climb out on the right side. At the top of the chute, go left (north). Continue north toward the obvious gully that leads to the top. Enter the gully on the right side as seen in Photo 5. If you hug the

Photo 1

east wall, you won't have a problem getting past the tight spot. The gully is a class I and II scramble. Scrambling up the right side of the gully is easiest.

A large boulder sits in the middle of the gully about halfway up; get around it by going to the left or right. A few yards past, three more boulders lie in the gully. A few yards past these boulders a path begins. Follow it to the right (east) for 10 to 20 yards. Turn left (north) and walk up to the top of the overlook. If you're at the

Ridgeline Rock

Bush

Photo 2

Jump Rock

Photo 3

correct spot, you'll be looking down on a picnic area and a gravel parking lot. To see Las Vegas, walk to the right (east) about 75 yards and look to your left for a concave boulder with a red, white, and blue painting. Climb to the left of this boulder and look out toward the east. The homes below are part of Calico Basin, and farther off is Las Vegas.

To Descend: You want to retrace your steps; however, since the sandstone starts to look the same, your steps are hard to retrace. Hike down the gully toward the narrow part. (See Photo 5.) Once past the narrow part, look for the yucca plant that sits to the left of the chute. (See Photo 6.) Also notice the large rock to the left of the yucca in Photo 6. Go to the far side of the chute and climb into it. Once down the chute go across the dirt, up the sandstone, and turn left onto a dirt path. When the path deadends into a massive wall of sandstone, turn right (west) into the alleyway. If you can see the gravel trail, you're headed in the correct direction. Follow the alleyway to Jump Rock. Climb up the sandstone slab on the other side of Jump Rock. From here

Photo 4

you can see the gravel trail and the wash. Cross the wash and scramble up the sandstone to the gravel trail.

Photo 5

Photo 6

♦ ♦ ♦

Calico Hills I Peak

Hike: Calico Hills I Peak — up and back
Trailhead: Calico Hills I parking lot — marked
Distance: 2 miles — round trip
Elevation gain: 750 feet
Elevation peak: 4,450 feet
Time: 2 hours
Difficulty: 2
Danger level: 2
How easy to follow: 5
Children: yes
Map: La Madre Mtn., NEV

Directions: The signed pulloff for Calico Hills I Overlook is located about one mile past the Scenic Loop gate.

Overview: The **route** goes across the wash, into the correct gully, and up a crack that leads to the peak.

Peak

Comments: This is one of the easier rock-scrambling routes. There is one semi-tough section, but it's not exposed. Turn around to see what the chutes and gullies will look like when you come down. Photo 1 shows the peak and an overview of the route.

Photo 1

The Hike: Descend NE down the

gravel trail onto the sandstone. Turn right going between the sandstone boulders
and scramble down the sandstone slabs until you see the
wash. Cross the wash and
hike east diagonally up the
sandstone ledges. (See Photo
2.) To the east a large boulder
sits on the ridgeline. This
boulder is called Ridgeline
Rock. (See Photo 3.) The trick
is to head in the direction of
Ridgeline Rock until you
come to the "U"-notch window in the sandstone alleyway (about 18 yards).

Photo 2

Climb down the sand-
stone slab and either leap onto Jump Rock and over to the next
sandstone slab, or climb down and around Jump Rock. (See
Photo 4.) Scramble up the sandstone slab and walk about halfway through the sandstone alleyway to a flat-bottom "U"-

Ridgeline Rock

Photo 3

notch window on the left
(north) side. Climb over the
window and head north (350
degrees) toward a false chute
by crisscrossing up the sandstone. (See Photo 5.) Stay in
front (south) of the false chute
and climb down the sandstone
boulders that lie partially hidden by scrub oak. Go onto the
path that passes in front of the
false chute and follow it as it
heads west in front of the
black-faced crags to an obvious
gully. (See Photo 6.) Scramble
near the right wall of the gully
and cross over onto the beehive

Photo 4

sandstone as outlined in Photo 7. Climb up the beehive sandstone about 40 feet and cross over onto a flat area to the crack. Climb up and around the boulder stuck in the crack. (See Photo 8.) This is the only difficult climb in the hike. Once at the top of the crack, look up to the highest point to see the name "Gary" etched into a huge black-faced boulder. (See Photo 9.) This is your next destination.

Scramble up to the chute that leads to the boulder with the name Gary. Once through the chute, head NW (340 degrees) to a boulder that has a small overhang on the left side. (See Photo 10.) From here you can see the black-faced boulder that is the peak. Head east (70 degrees), going between the black-faced boulder and the boulder to the right. There is no a cairn or sign-in book, but the view is remarkable; you are at the highest point in Calico Hills I.

To Descend: Although you will descend by the same route, it might be hard to recognize some of the gullies and chutes. From the peak head toward the visible Calico I parking lot. Once the sandstone flattens out, head left (east) and go in front of the Gary rock. Keep going east to the first chute that heads down toward the parking lot. Once

Photo 5

out of the chute, look for Ridgeline Rock, which is to the east. When it is directly across from you, find the parallel cracks and climb down the one that's nearest. This is the crack that the boulder lies in. The crack empties into the gully. Once out of the gully go left (east) alongside the black-faced crags to the path that goes in front of the false chute. When you are on the other side of the false chute, head south about 170 degrees toward the "U"-notch window. Climb over the "U"-

Photo 6

notch window and go right (west) in the alleyway to Jump Rock. Once on the crag that lies on the far side of Jump Rock, you can see the gravel trail and the parking lot.

Photo 7

Photo 8

Photo 9

Photo 10

◆ ◆ ◆

Calico Hills II Overlook

Hike: Calico Hills II Overlook — up and back
Trailhead: Calico Hills II Overlook — marked
Distance: 2 miles — round trip
Elevation gain: 600 feet
Elevation peak: 4,600 feet
Time: 2 hours
Difficulty: 3
Danger level: 3
How easy to follow: 4
Children: no
Map: La Madre Mtn., NEV

Directions: The signed pulloff for Calico Hills II Overlook is located 1.7 miles past the Scenic Loop gate.

Overview: The **route** goes down the **trail**, across the wash, and up the gully to the overlook.

Comments: This is a good bouldering route that leads to the best overlook in Calico Hills.

The Hike: From the signed trailhead, the trail descends rapidly toward the wash. When the trail forks, take the first right, then the first left. The trail sinks into the wash, which follows along three catch basins. At the top of the third catch basin, the path resumes. It soon splinters, but most of the paths lead to the gully. (Photo 1 shows the gully from the trailhead.)

Although unlikely, the catch basins might be filled with water. If they are, scramble up the sandstone mound to the left (west) of the catch basins. Continue toward the gully and climb down the sandstone onto any of the numerous paths that lead to the gully.

Once in the gully stay near the left (west) wall. About halfway up the gully you can follow a vague path or go to the right (east) side of the gully and scramble your way to the saddle.

At the saddle the path rambles to the left (NW) to a chute. (See Photo 2.) Photo 3 shows the boulder that divides the chute into right and left routes. The route to the left is easier and quicker. About halfway up the left route, a large boulder with a

Photo 1

white line running across it blocks the chute. Either climb up the rocks to the left of the boulder and then over it, or climb to the base of the boulder and step around the bush to the right

of it. Both ways meet at the other side. At the top of the chute the sandstone turns from red to white. A dirt path in a long alleyway lies between the sandstone mounds. From here, the idea is to head south toward the Scenic Loop. To do this, find the ramp that leads to the top of the white sandstone on the south side of the alleyway. Walk up the ramp and down the other side of the sandstone. Look for the juniper in Photo 4.

Crisscross the sandstone ramps on the far side of the juniper to the catch basin. From here, walk up

Photo 2

Photo 3

the ramp in Photo 5. Head for the highest point on the sandstone. When you see the words "Scout Troop 64 - 1963" written into the sandstone, you've made it to the top.

To Descend: Retrace your steps.

Juniper

Photo 4

Photo 5

♦ ♦ ♦

Calico Hills II Scramble

Hike: Calico Hills II Scramble — up and back
Trailhead: Calico II pulloff — marked
Distance: 2 miles — round trip
Elevation gain: 1,000 feet
Elevation peak: 5,000 feet
Time: 2 hours
Difficulty: 4
Danger level: 3
How easy to follow: 4
Children: no
Map: La Madre Mtn., NEV

Directions: The signed pulloff for Calico Hills II Overlook is located 1.7 miles past the Scenic Loop gate.

Overview: The **route** goes down the **trail**, up the wash, and into a gully. About halfway up the gully, the route heads east into another gully that leads to the top.

Comments: A short scramble loaded with enjoyable class II and class III scrambling.

The Hike: From the signed trailhead, the trail descends rapidly toward the wash. When the trail forks, take the first right, then the first left. As the trail sinks into the wash, follow as it passes alongside three catch basins. At the top of the third catch basin the path resumes. It begins to splinter, but most of the forks lead to the gully. If the catch basins are filled with water, scramble up the sandstone to the left (west) of the catch basins. Continue toward the gully, and climb down the sandstone and onto any of the numerous paths that lead to the gully.

Photo 1

Once in the gully, stay near the left (west) wall, climbing on the sandstone. About halfway up, an obvious gully comes in from the right (E). A large pinon pine stands at the entrance to the gully. Scramble toward the pine as indicated in Photo 1. Once near the pine, look for an obscure path that heads toward the pine; you'll avoid most of the scrub oak. Hike about 40 yards along a sandstone ledge on the left wall of the gully, then drop down into the gully. You'll be heading east.

Photo 2 shows the boulders that block the gully and the ledge system you climb to get around them. Zigzag back and forth on the ledges until you're past the boulders. In about 40 yards, another set of boulders blocks the gully. Very small hikers can go under the left-most boulder. The rest of us must climb over the boulders. (See Photo 3.) Once past this second obstacle, it's a short tromp up the gully, then up the sloping left wall to an area of level sandstone. From this point you'll see the second gully. (See Photo 4.)

Photo 2

The easiest way to the second gully is to climb down the

sandstone and go left until you see a pine tree (about 20 feet away). Drop down into a slickrock passage that lies below the pine. Head right and stay in the passage until it takes you to the start of the second gully. Turn left into the gully and hike along a ledge on the left side of it. Climb between two fallen

Photo 3

boulders when the gully seems blocked by numerous boulders. Shortly, you'll hike to the left of a cluster of scrub oak. When boulders again block the gully, go onto the ledge sys-

Peak

Photo 4

tem on the left (north) wall. Zigzag up the ledges and past the boulders. Near the top of the gully, cross to the right side and onto the staircase-like rock formation. (See Photo 5.) Climb up the staircase-like formation, then go left (60 degrees) in front of a large boulder and past more scrub oak. Look for the gutter-like formation; it'll be on your right. (See Photo 6.) Scramble up the gutter and watch for a crack at the top of the gutter as shown in Photo 7. Climb about six feet up the crack, then climb out on the right. Scramble to the top of the dome-shaped peak by crisscrossing on the beehive sandstone. A cairn might be at the peak. At the peak you're rewarded with good views of the Scenic Loop and Las Vegas.

To descend: Retrace your steps.

Photo 5

Photo 6   Photo 7

◆　◆　◆

Turtlehead Peak

Hike: Turtlehead Peak — up and back
Trailhead: Sandstone Quarry — marked
Distance: 5 miles — round trip
Elevation gain: 1,900 feet
Elevation peak: 6,323 feet
Time: 4 to 5 hours
Difficulty: 4
Danger level: 3
How easy to follow: 5
Children: no
Map: La Madre, NEV

Directions: The signed pulloff for Sandstone Quarry is located 2.8 miles past the Scenic Loop gate. The signed trailhead is at the far end of the parking lot.

Overview: The **route** follows a wash north through Calico Hills, climbs a chute to the west of Turtlehead Peak, and follows the ridge to the peak.

Comments: This is a good hike to test your fitness level. Great views of Las Vegas, Bridge Mountain, and the Scenic Loop are seen at the peak. Rattlesnakes have been seen (and heard) on this hike—be careful! This hike can be done during the summer months if you start early. Most of the route is in the shade during the early morning hours.

The Hike: As the gravel path begins in a NW direction, head toward a large cream-colored rock about 300 yards ahead. The trail empties into a large wash and disappears. Keep to the right of the large sandstone boulders that resemble oversized children's blocks. The wash pauses as you walk across a 50-foot section of cream-colored sandstone. At the end of the sandstone, the gravel wash continues. Photo 1 shows Turtlehead Peak and the trailhead.

Photo 1

About 200 yards ahead, a well-defined trail forms in the wash as rocks mark the boundary. The trail heads north into a dry creekbed making it easy to follow. About 100 yards up go left (west) at the first wash that heads west. The wash turns into a narrow sandstone slickrock passage and you encounter the first spot in which you must use class III climbing skills. In about 50 yards, they're used again to climb out of the narrow slickrock passage and into a dry wash. Once out of the passage, go to the left side of the whitish sandstone. Cross over to the right in about 20 yards and continue in the wash. The wash is broken up intermittently by sandstone slabs that are easily navigated. As the wash turns toward the south, Turtlehead Peak will be on your right at the one or two o'clock position.

Photo 2

When the wash appears to end, look for the juniper in Photo 2 and go to the right of it onto a faint path that heads in a SW direction. In 50 to 60 yards, the path empties into another wash. Go right at the gravel wash. At this point, Turtlehead

Peak is at the two o'clock position. The wash passes 60 yards to the left (south) of a small ridge. Just beyond this point, the wash looks as though it deadends. Go left up the limestone rock and continue in the wash.

Photo 3

The wash looks like it deadends into a nine-foot limestone wall. The center of the wall is slick; however, there are good holds a few feet to the right. Once up, continue in the wash until it looks like it is blocked by large rocks, then go to the left and continue to climb. Cairns mark the way. The path drops into a wash again and is easy to follow. As the wash splits and many paths begin to emerge, your landmark is the rock pinnacle in Photo 3. You want to head to the right of it and into the farthest right chute. The grade becomes steep as you make your way to the chute. When you see the slanted juniper in Photo 4, follow the dirt path that heads left (west). If you're in the correct wash, you'll come to a scrub oak that blocks the wash. Go to the right of it and then back into the wash. Photo 5 shows the tree that marks the beginning of the chute. Once in the chute, stay near the right (east) wall and climb until you see a 15-foot-tall pinion pine.

Photo 4

Go right (east) up the obvious path until it deadends into the wall. Go left (north) hugging the wall and climb to the top of the chute. At the top of the chute, head right (east) toward the peak. A vague path travels a quarter mile to the peak. On a clear day Las Vegas sparkles and Lake Mead is visible farther to the east.

To Descend: Follow the ridgeline until it flattens out. The chute you just climbed is at the beginning of the flat area.

Photo 5

◆　◆　◆

Turtlehead Jr.

Hike: Turtlehead Jr. — up and back
Trailhead: Sandstone Quarry — marked
Distance: 3 miles — round trip
Elevation gain: 1,100 feet
Elevation peak: 5,443 feet
Time: 2 hours
Difficulty: 3
Danger level: 4
How hard to follow: 5
Children: no
Map: La Madre, NEV

Directions: The signed pulloff for Sandstone Quarry is located 2.8 miles past the Scenic Loop gate. The signed trailhead is at the far end of the parking lot.

Overview: There is a 30-minute approach hike before the climb begins. The **route** is a series of class II and III cracks and chutes.

Comments: If you are looking for a short but challenging scramble, this is it. Turtlehead Jr. is one of the highest points on the sandstone on the north side of the Scenic Loop. Photo 1 shows the top of Turtlehead Jr. It cannot be seen from the trailhead. You can hike this route in the summer if you get an early start. This is a good test hike before attempting the Bridge Mountain hike.

The Hike: As the gravel trail begins in a NW direction, head toward a large cream-colored crag about 300 yards ahead. The trail empties into a large wash and disappears. Stay to the right of the large sandstone boulders that resemble oversized children's blocks. The wash pauses as you walk across a 50-foot section of cream-colored sandstone. At the end of the sandstone the gravel wash continues. Stay in the middle of the wash and continue in a NW direction. You'll pass a section of cream-colored sandstone that jets into the wash. Stop and look up to your right; in the distance is a huge cream-colored sandstone crag with a crack running diagonally from the lower left to the upper right. This crag, called Blister in the Sun Cliff, is your

Photo 1

first destination. At the top of Blister in the Sun Cliff is a red-colored dome. This is Turtlehead Jr. Peak, your final destination.

Continue in the wash until a well-defined trail heads right (north) and goes into a dry creekbed. The sides of the trail are marked by rocks. Once in the creekbed, Turtlehead Jr. lies in front of you. The trail passes over a large slab of red sandstone and proceeds through a narrow passage with a bush in the middle. (See Photo 2.)

As the creekbed bends to the left, take the dirt path that comes in from the right. It heads toward Blister in the Sun Cliff. The dirt path crosses a red sandstone slab. To the left is a large, overhanging, cream-colored sandstone formation. Walk

Photo 2

Blister in the Sun Cliff

Photo 3

along the base of the formation and follow the dirt path until it deadends.

Scramble up the sandstone toward Blister in the Sun Cliff. This is a strenuous but safe class I and II climb. Once up to the base of Blister in the Sun Cliff, head SE parallel to it (40 degrees). Ahead stands a sandstone crag; to the left is a larger sandstone crag with a vertical crack and a bush about halfway up the crack. Climb to the left of the white line in Photo 4. This is where the class III climb begins. Climb to the right of the first crack. At the flat part (about 45 feet), go to the left and continue climbing (about 50 feet) until you come to the bush. Climb past the bush to the top of the crack. At the top, climb to the right onto the buttress. Once on top of the buttress, carefully step over the crack you just climbed. Walk about 25 feet till you see a chute on your right. As the chute narrows, climb to the right of it, then climb back into the chute once it widens. You'll see an eight-foot boulder on its side blocking the chute; climb to the left of the boulder and continue up the chute. At the top of the chute, the sandstone flattens out into a large area. To the left is an enormous cream-colored sandstone crag. To the right are a

Bush

Photo 4

few bushes and trees. Walk NE toward this enormous sandstone crag. A couple of feet before the crag lies a large opening on the left side. Go up this opening. The opening narrows toward the end; large people may have a tight squeeze. At the top of the opening are three cracks—you must climb one of these (class III).

At the top of the cracks, the sandstone turns from cream to red in color. Head almost due east toward the top of Turtlehead Jr. Go across a section of rock chips, then by two dry catch basins. For the final ascent, climb the crack in Photo 5. A small bush grows at the top of this crack. Once past the bush, run up the steep slope to the top of Turtlehead Jr. To the west lies Turtlehead Peak, to the east is Las Vegas, and to the SW is the Scenic Loop and Bridge Mountain.

Photo 5

To Descend: Although you will descend by the same route, the sandstone looks amazingly similar and it's easy to get confused. Climb down the crack and head toward Turtlehead Peak, passing the dry catch basins and the rock chips. Once you see the sandstone change from red to cream, go left and look for the crack you climbed up. Go down the narrow opening. From there, turn right (south) and walk toward the bushes. Look for the chute that has the boulder blocking it. Climb down the chute and around the boulder. Do not go to the left until you can no longer climb down the chute. Walk to the left, crossing over the crack and onto the buttress. Climb down into the crack toward the bush. At the bush, go left (south) and walk down the beehive sandstone. Toward the bottom, look for the final crack. It will be on your left. After climbing down the final crack, you'll be at the base of Blister in the Sun Cliff. Stay near the base and head NW toward the gravel rockbed. Near the bottom, head SW and look for the gravel bed. Follow the gravel bed until a faint dirt path appears to the left. Follow this path, which passes by the base of the overhanging formation. The dirt path disappears, then starts up again. Follow it until it dumps you into the creekbed. Go left into the creekbed and follow it to the trailhead.

◆　◆　◆

Calico Tanks

Hike: Calico Tanks — up and back
Trailhead: Sandstone Quarry — marked
Distance: 3 miles — round trip
Elevation gain: 450 feet
Elevation peak: 5,022
Time: 3 to 5 hours
Difficulty: 3
Danger level: 2
How easy to follow: 4
Children: yes
Map: La Madre Mtn., NEV

Directions: The signed pulloff for Sandstone Quarry is located 2.8 miles past the Scenic Loop gate. The marked trailhead is at the far end of the parking lot.

Overview: The **route** goes through a wash, empties into a dry creekbed, follows the creekbed, and goes up the sandstone to the tanks.

Comments: An amazing spectacle awaits you at the end of this route: a dry lake in the middle of the desert.

Hike: The gravel trail begins in a NW direction and you head toward a large cream-colored crag about 300 yards ahead. When you pass large sandstone boulders that look like over-sized children's blocks, keep to the right. The gravel disappears as you walk across a 50-foot section of sandstone, then reappears. Stay in the middle of the wash and continue NW. Ahead stands a much smaller cream-colored crag, about 50 to

75 feet high, with a noticeable crack running diagonally. A well-defined trail begins to form in the gravel with rocks marking its boundary. It heads into a dry creekbed and becomes easy to follow. The trail turns west, then two well-defined dirt trails head off in a NE direction. Follow the second trail. This short trail empties into another creekbed. Take the obvious paths to the right if there's water in the creekbed. The sandstone changes to a dark red, the creekbed turns sandy for 10 to 15 yards, then the sandstone reappears. When the creekbed splits, go either way; the forks rejoin after 50 yards. Perched high

Photo 1

up in the sandstone on the right side is a distinctive boulder. (See Photo 1.)

Head toward this boulder. A little farther along the creekbed, huge red boulders block the way. Go left of the boulders and scramble parallel to the creekbed. You'll come to a two-foot crack in the red sandstone; leap across or walk around to the far left. At this point the distinctive boulder is in view. Hike across the sand to a dry basin. Huge white boulders partially block the way—distinctive against the red sandstone. (See Photo 2.) Go to the left of the white boulders and continue in the creekbed.

Photo 3 shows where to make the 15-foot climb out of the

Photo 2

wash and marks the way to the top. Scramble the 50 yards across the red sandstone to a path that heads west (left). You're now at the bottom of a huge white sandstone mound that goes up to a saddle. A 10-foot white boulder, which looks like it slid

Photo 3

down from above, lies at the bottom of this huge mound. (See Photo 4.) A chute forms about 20 yards up from this boulder. (See Photo 5.)

Follow the chute up to the saddle where a dirt path forms. The Calico Tanks lie on the other side of the sandstone wall in front of you. The easiest way around is to head toward the boulder in Photo 6.

The best way to get to this boulder is to hike down across the

Photo 4

sand and dirt, around the scrub oak, and onto the sandstone. Once around the boulder, head NNE (20 degrees) down into the dirt and sand. This lowland is called Calico Tanks Passage. All three Calico Tanks are close by. Look to your left down the passage and you'll see a fallen tree. You are actually in the passage at this point; it runs west to east. Walk toward the fallen tree and go right at the obvious crack that leads up to Tank 1. (See Photo 7.) Once at the top, walk to the right. The first tank is almost 75 feet deep. Depending on the rainfall, there might be water at the bottom. Retrace your steps back to the passage and go east (110 degrees) to the second Tank. Tank

1 and Tank 2 are about 200 yards apart. At the SE corner of Tank 2, a short passage leads to Tank 3. If you want to climb down into Tank 3, stay in the passage and go between the dead-looking tree and the sandstone. Do not go around the tree—it's too brushy.

It's amazing to see a dry lakebed in the barren sandstone, but this is only one of the unexpected sights that await you at Red Rock Canyon. The more you hike in this playground, the more your mind will be boggled.

If you hike down into this tank, remember the passage is in the NE corner of the lake bed.

To Descend: Retrace your steps.

Photo 6

Photo 5

Photo 7

Grand Circle West

Hike: Grand Circle West — closed loop
Trailhead: Keystone Thrust — marked
Distance: 7 miles
Elevation gain: 700 feet
Elevation peak: no peak
Time: 3 to 4 hours
Difficulty: 2
Danger level: 1
How easy to follow: 4
Children: yes
Map: La Madre Mtn., NEV

Directions: The signed turnoff for White Rock Springs is located 5.8 miles past the Scenic Loop gate. Turn right at the sign and either park at the lower parking lot or drive and park at the upper parking lot. The trailhead is located at the upper parking lot. Starting the hike at the lower parking lot adds slightly more than a half mile to the hike.

Overview: The **route** heads toward La Madre Mountain before dropping into a wash that goes to Sandstone Quarry. From the Quarry, the **route** follows part of the Grand Circle Trail to return to White Rock Springs.

Comments: The hike takes you past the Keystone Thrust fault and into the limestone regions of Red Rock. This is one of the longest and easiest hikes in Red Rock. The first mile and a half of the route follows the Keystone Thrust Trail (see p. 139).

The Hike: The trail starts off at a slight incline as it heads due

Photo 1

north. It soon passes a signed roasting pit. The trail crosses a wash and comes to a fork. Take the right fork and continue toward the fault line. When the trail comes to an intersection, go left and head toward Cactus Hill. (See Photo 1). The incline is slight to moderate as you continue north. The trail deadends into an abandoned gravel road. Go left onto the road and proceed toward Cactus Hill. As the road flattens out, it heads south (left) of Cactus Hill. The incline increases as the gravel road passes Cactus Hill.

The gravel road deteriorates into a path as it passes an unnamed dolomite hill. As the path makes its way toward a saddle, look for small cairns that mark the way. The path becomes hard to follow as it goes by a four-foot stump. Veer left of the stump and look for a cairn that marks the continuation of the path. Head north (20 degrees) toward La Madre Mountain; you'll come to the top of a foothill. (See Photo 2.) Gray rock covering the ground makes the path hard to follow. Go around to the backside of the foothill that you've just hiked.

Photo 2

Look for cairns that mark the path's descent into a creekbed. The path goes into the creekbed, but doesn't cross to the other side. Stay in the creekbed, head NE (right), and watch for the cairns. When bushes or boulders block the path in the creekbed, look for side paths that go up and around on the right side. The creekbed deadends into a wash. Go east (right) into the wash and continue to follow the cairns. At this point the path has vanished and the hike turns into a route.

The route heads east, and you can see the sandstone crags of Sandstone Quarry. Off to the left is Turtlehead Peak as seen in Photo 3. The wash widens as the route sinks down toward Sandstone Quarry. Eventually, sandstone crags appear as the wash narrows. The wash widens after passing between the sandstone crags.

Turtlehead Peak

Photo 3

Shortly after this point you can see Sandstone Quarry parking lot and the Scenic Loop road. The route deadends into the Sandstone Quarry Trail. Go right (south) onto the Sandstone Quarry Trail. It passes by sandstone blocks that were discarded years ago by the quarry. Rocks outline the trail as it crosses a wash. Follow the trail past the boulders and look for a small sign off to the right marking the Grand Circle Trail. Go right (south) on the Grand Circle Trail.

This trail crosses a wash as it heads SW toward a minor hill, then crosses the Scenic Loop road and heads SW. When it drops down into another wash, look for the juniper that marks the continuation of the trail. Cross the Scenic Loop again and follow White Rock Springs Road to the parking lot.

◆ ◆ ◆

Keystone Thrust

Hike: Keystone Thrust — up and back
Trailhead: White Rock Springs — marked
Distance: 3 miles — round trip
Elevation gain: 542 feet
Elevation peak: none
Time: 2 hours
Difficulty: 1
Danger level: 1
How easy to follow: 1
Children: yes
Map: La Madre Mtn., NEV

Directions: The signed turnoff road for White Rock Springs is located 5.8 miles past the Scenic Loop gate. Turn right and either park at the lower lot or drive a half mile and park at the upper lot. The trailhead is located at the upper parking lot.

Overview: The **trail** crosses a wash and climbs a hill before descending to the fault.

Comments: This trail is the shortest hike that leads to the famous Keystone Thrust fault line.

The Hike: The trail starts off at a slight incline as it heads due north. It soon passes a roasting pit, which is marked by a BLM sign. The trail crosses a wash and comes to a fork. Take the right fork and continue toward the fault line. When the trail comes to an intersection, go left and head toward the gray dolomite mountain, called Cactus Hill. (See Photo 1.) The incline is slight to moderate as the trail continues to head north.

Photo 1

When the trail deadends into an abandoned gravel road, go left and hike toward Cactus Hill. The trail flattens out as it heads to the left (south) of Cactus Hill. The incline becomes slight to moderate as the trail passes Cactus Hill. When you reach the top of an unnamed hill you've been climbing, turn right (north) and descend about 200 yards to the Keystone fault

Photo 2

line. (See photo 2.) The fault line is marked by the sandstone on the east side and the gray dolomite and green vegetation on the west side. Geologists come from all over the world to study the fault line.

To Descend: Retrace your steps.

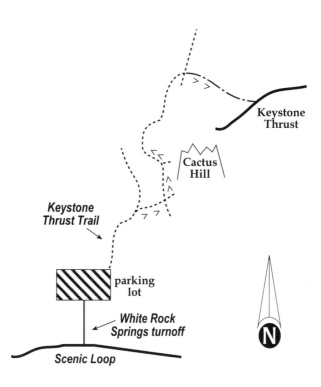

◆ ◆ ◆

White Rock Springs Peak

Hike: White Rock Springs Peak — up and back
Trailhead: White Rock/Willow Springs/La Madre — marked
Distance: 5 miles — round trip
Elevation gain: 1,203 feet
Elevation peak: 5,977 feet
Time: 3.5 hours
Difficulty: 3
Danger level: 3
How easy to follow: 3
Children: no
Map: La Madre Mtn., NEV

Directions: The signed turnoff road for White Rock Springs is located 5.8 miles past the Scenic Loop gate. Turn right and park in the lower lot or drive a half mile to the upper lot, where the trailhead is located.

Overview: Follow the **trail** to the cutoff point, then it's a **route** across the desert and up to the peak.

Comments: This scrambling route is similar to the longer scrambling hikes in Red Rock. Before trying those hikes, you should do this hike to see how you fare. This peak appears to be an easy climb from the trailhead, but by the time you reach the top, you'll feel like you've climbed a mountain.

The Hike: The trail begins at the SW corner of the parking lot. Follow it for about 100 yards, then go left at the fork onto the abandoned dirt road. This part of the trail has a slight decline as it passes east of White Rock Springs Peak. (See Photo 1.) Once you're about even with the peak, leave the trail and head west (300 degrees) toward the peak. It's easy to avoid the scrub oak by weaving around it. You'll cross a large wash as you hike across the desert. Beyond the first wash, you'll cross two more minor washes. From this vantage point you can see many chutes up to the peak.

Photo 1

The idea is to hike up a wash and then up the northernmost chute as delineated in Photo 2. You'll cross one last wash, marked by reddish dirt on its northern end, before the route takes a definite course. Photo 2 shows the sandstone crag; stay to the right (north) of it. You do this by eventually dropping into the wash and climbing past the sandstone crag. The wash, though a more direct route, is brushy in the lower parts. The walk-up on the south side of the wash looks easy; however, the top is filled with brush. Once in the wash, you'll encounter a small section of easy class III climbing as seen in Photo 3. It's easier to climb up on the left (south) side. Past the class III climb, the wash heads west and the climbing is class II.

Photo 2

About 75 yards after the class III climb, a large mound of pinkish-white sandstone sits on the south side of the wash. This mound becomes a major landmark for the descent. The peak is visible from this point. Photo 4 highlights which chute you should climb to reach the peak. There is no correct way to get to the chute; however, you'll cross two washes. Go up the second wash NW (335 degrees) until it starts to disappear. If

Photo 3

you're in the correct wash, you'll climb past a tree that has fallen into the wash. Once the wash fades, make your way to the base of the chute. The incline is strenuous.

Climbing the sandstone wash at the base of the chute is easy and your ascent is rapid. Once the wash stops, the chute becomes dirt and rock with patches of brush, which will influence your decision on choosing the best route. Generally, it's better to keep to the right side of the chute as you make your way toward the right (north) side of the pinnacle seen in Photo 5. At the top of the chute you'll be able to see La Madre Mountain to the west. It's a good idea to make a small cairn marking this chute for

Photo 4

the descent, since you'll pass a number of chutes before you reach the peak.

Turn to the left (south) to see White Springs Peak. Head south in front of the sandstone crags until you get to the base of the peak. You need to descend about 100 feet below the ridgeline to get around one of the crags. (See Photo 6.) At the base of the peak, hike west back up to the ridgeline, then go to the backside of the peak. From this point the cairn that marks the peak is visible. Climb onto the giant sandstone blocks as you make your way SSW to the cairn.

To Descend: Head NE (30 degrees) down the backside of the peak. Descend off the east side of the ridgeline in front of the sandstone crags to the correct chute. Did you make a cairn marking it? Climb down the chute and head to the left (north) of the pinkish-white sandstone seen in Photo 7. Descend down the wash. From this point you can see the trail.

Photo 5

Photo 6

Photo 7

♦ ♦ ♦

La Madre Notch

Hike: La Madre Notch — up and back
Trailhead: Keystone Trail — marked
Distance: 7.5 miles — round trip
Elevation gain: 1,817 feet
Elevation peak: 6,691 feet
Time: 4 to 5 hours
Difficulty: 4
Danger level: 3
How easy to follow: 3
Children: no
Map: La Madre Mtn., NEV

Directions: The signed turnoff road for White Rock Springs is located 5.8 miles past the Scenic Loop gate. Turn right and either park at the lower parking lot or drive half a mile and park at the upper parking lot. The trailhead is located at the upper parking lot.

Overview: The hike follows the Keystone Thrust **trail** and the White Springs Trail, then it's a cross-country **route** up the wash that leads to the notch.

Comments: If you're looking for a Mt. Charleston-type hike in Red Rock, this is it. After leaving the trail, it's a hike/climb up a limestone ridge of La Madre Mountain. In two miles you climb more than 1,500 feet. Be extremely careful when descending on the talus. Hikers have sent huge rocks tumbling down the mountain. You should limit the number of hikers in your party to four due to the loose rock.

The Hike: The trail starts off with a slight incline as it heads due north. It soon passes a roasting pit, which is marked by a BLM sign. The trail crosses a wash and comes to a fork. Continue on the main trail; do not go right onto the Keystone Thrust Trail. As the trail heads NNW (340 degrees), it has a moderate incline. To the south lies White Rock Hills. The trail takes a SW direction as red sandstone crags of White Rock Hills become visible from the trail. These red sandstone crags will serve as a landmark when descending.

Photo 1

Once at the crest of the hill the trail has been climbing, stop and look toward the south. You're looking at the Keystone Thrust fault line. The younger sandstone to the left and the older limestone to the right are both the result of a major movement of land masses some 65 million years ago, which caused the older limestone to rise above the newer sandstone. Geologists from all over the world come to study this phenomenon. At this same overlook you can see the notch you will be climbing by looking NW (300 degrees—see Photo 1).

About 200 yards past the crest of the hill, the trail comes to a small dry wash. Just before the wash, a large limestone rock lies by the right side of the trail; this marks the point where you depart from the trail. Head NW (300 degrees) across the desert toward the notch in Photo 1. It's easy to avoid the brush during this trek across the desert. Although, you can't see it from this point, a major wash lies just before your ascent up the dry wash to the notch. This wash lies perpendicular and is about 75 feet deep. Wait to drop down into the wash until it's only a 30-foot descent. Go down the bank into the wash. Continue north in the wash until you see the minor wash that heads toward the notch; it's distinguishable by the whitish limestone. Brush fills the first 10 yards of the wash, which heads WSW (250 degrees) toward the notch. After the wash twists, you get a good view of the notch. When the wash comes to a six-foot wall, climb up the wall, or go to the left, hiking up and then crossing over above the wall. The wash is a class II hike. As the wash begins to narrow, it's quicker to follow it along the right (north) side. The incline at this point is moderate.

A deep gully begins to form to the right (north). Stay on its left (south) bank; do not drop down into the gully. The notch is about 300 yards away. (See Photo 2.) The incline becomes steep as you continue toward the notch, and the cliffs that form the notch close in.

Head toward the left (south) wall of the notch. Take the faint path that heads south toward the limestone wall; it avoids the limestone. Once at the left (south) wall, follow alongside it and climb up to the boulder field seen in Photo

Photo 2

3. Scramble up the steep boulder field. Near the top of the boulder field, to the left (south), is a bluff that overlooks Red Rock. Hike to the bluff. (See Photo 4.)

The next obstacle to gain is the cliff wall that was hidden until the bluff. From the bluff, head west (255 degrees), staying about 30 yards below the cliff wall. In about 100 yards another cliff forms; stay on top of it and continue westerly until the upper cliff wall ends by the juniper

Photo 3

Photo 4

in Photo 5. Climb up to the juniper and head toward the limestone pinnacles in Photo 6. At the limestone pinnacles, climb up the limestone by the bushes shown in Photo 7. Head ENE (75 degrees) to the top, which lies another 75 yards away. Unfortunately, no cairn or sign-in book marks the peak, but the view of Red Rock is awesome. If you are planning an exploratory hike to North Peak via Lost Creek, the view from this angle should help.

Photo 5

An obvious peak lies to the north of the peak you are currently on. If you plan to hike to it, you should have at least six hours of daylight left to return to the trailhead. Don't be fooled into thinking the bluff just below and to the right is the same bluff you were on in Photo 4. Below that bluff lies the 100-foot cliff wall you hiked around. The pinnacles you are now standing on can't be seen until you've reached the juniper in Photo 5.

To Descend: Retrace your steps. First, come down the pinnacles and go across to the juniper that marks the way down from the cliff. Stay near the cliff wall as you head east back to the bluff. At the bluff go north to the boulder field and descend heading to the right (south) wall of the notch. Follow the faint path down into the wash. Use the red sandstone in White Rock Hills as a landmark. You should be to the left (north) of them, descending SE (130 degrees). Once out of the wash, go right (south), into the major wash, then up the east bank of the wash. Head SE (150 degrees) across the desert to the trail. Go left onto the trail back to the trailhead.

Photo 6

Photo 7

♦   ♦   ♦

Goldfish Pond

Hike: Gold Fish Pond — up and back
Trailhead: White Rock/Willow Springs/La Madre — marked
Distance: less than a half mile — round trip
Elevation gain: none
Elevation peak: no peak
Time: 20 to 30 minutes
Difficulty: 1
Danger level: 1
How easy to follow: 1
Children: yes
Map: La Madre Mtn., NEV

Directions: The signed turnoff road for White Rock Springs is located 5.8 miles past the Scenic Loop gate. Turn right and park at either the lower parking lot or drive a half mile and park at the upper parking lot. The trailhead is located at the upper parking lot.

Overview: The **trail** leads to a pond with dozens of goldfish.

Comments: This is the shortest hike in the book. No one knows who put the goldfish in the pond.

The Hike: The trail begins at the SW corner of the parking lot. Follow it for about 100 yards and go right at the fork. The trail descends another 150 yards and stops at a concrete-bottom pond that's home to dozens of goldfish.

To Descend: Retrace your steps.

♦ ♦ ♦

White Rock Hills Loop

Hike: White Rock Hills loop — closed loop
Trailhead: White Rock/Willow Springs/La Madre — marked
Distance: 6.5 miles
Elevation gain: 788 feet
Elevation peak: no peak
Time: 3.5 hours
Difficulty: 2
Danger level: 1
How easy to follow: 1
Children: yes
Map: La Madre Mtn., NEV and La Madre Springs, NEV

Directions: The signed turnoff road for White Rock Springs is 5.8 miles past the Scenic Loop gate. Turn right and either park at the lower parking lot or drive a half mile to the upper parking lot. The trailhead is located at the upper parking lot.

Overview: The **trail** circles White Rock Hills.

Comments: Since this is a loop hike, you can begin at White Rock Springs or at Willow Springs. The trail is described clockwise. The hike is a composite of many different BLM trails.

The Hike: The trail begins at the SW corner of the parking lot. (The Keystone Trail begins in the NW corner, which is the ending point of this hike.) Follow the trail for about 100 yards and go left at the fork onto the abandoned dirt road. This part of the trail descends slightly as it passes east of White Rock Hills, then drops into a ravine. At the bottom of the ravine the trail goes left and weaves through a patch of bushes before climbing out. At the top of the ravine, the trail travels down into a depression where water collects, as is evident by the amount of trees and greenery.

A small ridge to the east is the trail's next destination. Once over the ridge the turnoff for the Grand Circle Trail comes in from the left (SE), but stay on this trail. Soon the paved road that goes to Willow Springs comes into view. The trail descends gently as it starts to head west toward Willow Springs parking area. Go right at the intersection; the trail parallels the road. If you go straight, you'll cross the road and be at the Lost Creek trailhead.

The trail crosses a concrete slab that is part of a BLM exhibit of an ancient roasting pit. Continue on the far side of the concrete; do not go left onto the spur trail. Once you pass a house-sized boulder, go left onto any path that leads the 30 yards to the Willow Springs parking lot. You have hiked about two miles at this point.

Walk to the west end of the Willow Springs parking lot and continue hiking on the Rocky Gap Road; it's unmarked, but a large sign reads, "Not a County Maintained Road." In about three-quarters of a mile, a BLM sign marks the start of the La Madre Springs Trail. Go right onto this trail as it heads north. The grade is mild. To the east lies the backside of White Rock Hills. The incline becomes moderate as the trail heads NW toward La Madre Spring. Make a right onto the trail that comes in from the right (east) side marked by three large boulders.

This part of the trail weaves NE around the backside of White Rock Hills. The incline is slight as the trail crosses a dry creekbed. It soon passes a small hill of brown rocks that looks out of place. When the trail passes the reddish sandstone in White Rock Hills, the incline becomes moderate. The trail climbs a small hill; at the top of the hill is a good view of Calico Hills to the east and the Rocky Gap Road to the south. As the trail heads ENE, it weaves around the north side of White Rock Hills. A gentle descent marks the last leg of the trail as it makes its way back to the White Rock Springs parking lot.

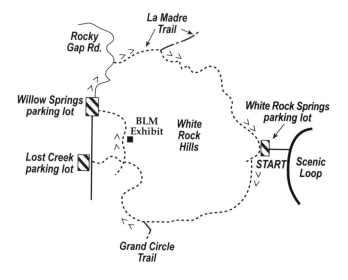

◆ ◆ ◆

White Rock Hills Peak

Hike: White Rock Hills Peak — up and back
Trailhead: Rocky Gap Road
Distance: 6 miles — round trip
Elevation gain: 1,862 feet
Elevation peak: 6,462 feet
Time: 6 to 8 hours
Difficulty: 5
Danger level: 5
How easy to follow: 5
Children: no
Map: La Madre Mtn., NEV

Directions: The signed turnoff for Willow Springs is located 7.3 miles past the Scenic Loop gate. It's a six-tenths-of-a-mile drive on the paved road to the gravel parking lot. Drive or walk four-tenths of a mile on the Rocky Gap Road. When the road bends to the right, look for the pine tree in Photo 1. Park on the opposite side of the road where the five large boulders sit. It's recommended to park at this spot so your car can serve as a landmark.

Overview: Hike straight up a sandstone mountain, negotiating a succession of ledges. The **route** goes up a dry waterfall, across a ridge, and finally there's a long scramble to the peak.

Comments: Only experienced hikers should attempt this route. There are some class III sections. Many hikers get stuck on this mountain. Look back often to spot landmarks you can use on the way back. Large hikers should not attempt this route; one chimney is very narrow. Think of this hike in three sec-

tions. The first section is a series of ledges that must be
climbed; the route is hard to
follow. The second section
goes to a dry waterfall and
over a saddle to a ridgeline.
This section is easier to follow.
The last section follows a path
to a passage and then up a
chute to the peak.

The Hike: Follow the steep
dirt path that goes to the im-
mediate right of the pinion
pine in Photo 1. The path
heads almost due north as it
passes between two junipers.
The path turns slightly to the

Photo 1

right and goes over white boulders with dark red circles before heading into a dry wash. Follow the wash until it comes
to a small cave. (See Photo 2.) About 30 feet before the cave,
the path goes to the right and climbs above the cave. Once

Photo 2

Photo 3

above the cave, turn around and face the Rocky Gap Road. The pinion pine that marks the trailhead should be directly in front of you.

Continue hiking up the wash. The route leads into the white sandstone. Ahead lies a 30-foot wall of sandstone with dark gray water streaks running down its face. On top of this wall sits a thin mantle-like rock. This is your next destination. (See Photo 3.) Walk to the left (WNW) about 30 yards on the ledge until it diminishes. At this point, it's an easy climb to the next level of sandstone. Walk to the right (east), up the ramp that takes you above the wall and to the thin mantle-like rock.

From the mantle-like rock, head slightly to the left, by the bushes, and scramble up to the next level of sandstone, climbing up the rock as shown in Photo 4. Head east (right)

Photo 4

Photo 5

along the ledge until it drops off and scramble up to the next level of sandstone to a thin dead tree about six feet tall. Walk east past the dead tree and the scrub oak, then scramble up the sandstone to another cave. Climb the crack that's to the right (east) of the cave. The arrow in Photo 5 points toward the crack. Once above the cave, head toward a patch of beavertail cacti. From the cacti, hike toward the wash surrounded by scrub oak and junipers. (See Photo 6.) Hike up the wash. When you encounter the next sandstone wall, go to the left and zigzag

Photo 6

Photo 7

above the wall.

Photo 7 shows a dead tree at the top of another sandstone wall. This is your next destination. To get to the tree, walk up on the left side, between a half-dead juniper and the wall. (See Photo 8.) Continue to the left and climb up a crack to a large juniper and a log that lies next to the juni-per. A cairn sits at the top of the crack. You are now at the top of the wall. The dead tree in Photo 7 is about 40 yards to the east. About 10 yards before the dead tree, look for the chute in Photo 9. It will be to your left. Climb up the chute. Go right (east) to a patch of scrub oak and manzanita bushes. Be-

Photo 8

hind the bushes is a wall with enough hand and foot holds to climb.

Once at the top of the wall, head to your left (NW) for about 100 yards and climb up the chimney in Photo 10. Be careful climbing out of the chimney onto the sandstone ledge. Once out of the chimney, head right (east) toward the passage. Walk up the left side of the passage to the top. At the top of the passage, head left and walk up past the pine tree to the top (80 degrees) where refrigerator-sized

Photo 9

boulders rest. This marks the end of the first section of the hike.

Photo 10

A large cave-like structure lies about 100 yards to the east. (See Photo 11.) Head toward the cave-like structure. To the left of the cave-like structure lies a dry waterfall. Climb up the center of the waterfall. (See Photo 12.)

Once above the dry waterfall, follow the faint path that heads almost due north (10 degrees) to the saddle that lies between the two crags. It's about 100 yards from the dry waterfall to the saddle. (See Photo 13.)

Notice the pine tree growing out of the side of the

Photo 11

Photo 12

Photo 13

sandstone in Photo 13. A cairn marks the top of the saddle. A large puzzle-shaped rock lies above the saddle on the left side. This helps locate the saddle on the way back. Once on the other side of the saddle, turn right (north) and stay on the boulders. Cairns mark the way as you scramble up and down the sandstone boulders. Once you reach the flat sandstone, head north toward the dead tree that sits on the ridgeline. (See Photo 14.) Look for cairns that mark the route. Go to the east (right) of the dead tree, past manzanita bushes, then scramble up the sandstone slabs.

Photo 14

Watch for cairns that mark the way to the pine trees that rest on the ridgeline. At the pine trees, the peak can been seen to the NE. (See Photo 15.) This ends the second section of the hike.

Photo 15

As you look at the land below the peak, you see three levels that you can traverse to get to the peak. The idea is to hike down to the lowest level and across to a dry wash that can't be seen from this vantage point. Start by walking to the left (west) of the crags and finding the path that eventually leads to the wash. At this point, you are hiking on the top level. Look for a 15-foot log that has fallen against a

Photo 16

boulder. This marks your descent to the middle level. Climb down on the right side of the log and follow the pine-needle path that leads to the peak. In about 75 to 100 yards, the path drops down to the lowest level, allowing you to avoid the limestone-looking pinnacles that lie directly ahead. When the path starts to go over a rock avalanche area, look for the dry wash above and scramble up the right side of the wash. (See Photo 16.) Look for the huge pine tree that marks the beginning of the passage. (See Photo 17.) Walk to the top of the passage and turn left. A cairn sits at the top of the passage. Head NE (50 degrees) staying to the right as you scramble up the sandstone.

Cairns mark the easiest route. Photo 18 shows the chute that takes you to the peak. The chute is about 80 yards from the top of the passage. When the chute looks like it stops, climb to the left under an overhanging rock. At the top of the chute, look to the left; the peak is visible.

Hike about 20 yards to a slab of sandstone that blocks the way. Go right, hiking in front of this slab. Once past, look to the left; the peak lies 30 yards away. Climb to the peak in Photo

Huge Pine Tree →

Photo 17

Photo 18

19. The peak offers one of the best views of Red Rock Canyon. You also get an appreciation of the size of White Rock Mountain.

To Descend: Hike down the chute to the passage. Go down the passage and the wash to the path. Look toward the SW (240 degrees) for the dead tree on the ridgeline. (See Photo 14.) To get to the dead tree, you'll have to hike up to the top level; you are currently on the lowest level. Follow the path and watch for the dead log that you climbed down. Climb up on the right side of the log (this is the opposite side from where you climbed down) and hike across to the pine tree. Scramble down the sandstone slabs looking for cairns that outline the easiest route. Once down to the flat area, look for the puzzle rock. The saddle sits below. Climb over the saddle and down the path to the waterfall. At the bottom of the wa-

terfall, look toward the SW for a large crag. The crag marks the top of the passage that lies above the narrow chimney. You didn't forget the narrow chimney, did you? From this point you can see your car. Follow the first section of the hike in reverse to get back to the trailhead.

Photo 19

♦ ♦ ♦

Lost Creek Canyon/
Children's Discovery Trail

Hike: Lost Creek Canyon/Children's Discovery Trail
— up and back or closed loop
Trailhead: Willow Springs Picnic Area — marked
Distance: 1 mile — round trip
Elevation gain: 240 feet
Elevation peak: no peak
Time: 40 minutes
Difficulty: 1
Danger level: 1
How easy to follow: 1
Children: yes
Map: La Madre Mtn., NEV

Directions: The signed turnoff for Willow Springs is located 7.3 miles past the Scenic Loop gate. Lost Creek parking area is a fifth-of-a-mile drive from the Scenic Loop.

Overview: The **trail** heads south to the mouth of Lost Creek Canyon. A short trail leads to a waterfall. The trail then loops back to the west onto the Children's Discovery Trail.

Comments: This is a great beginner's hike. The seasonal waterfall is spectacular, considering it's in the desert. You can start at either trailhead, since they form a loop.

The Hike: The Lost Creek Trail heads SW toward the mouth of Lost Creek. The incline remains almost flat the entire hike. In about 50 yards the trail climbs enough to see the greenery near the mouth of the canyon. This is an unexpected sight in the middle of the desert. The trail crosses Red Rock Wash and goes up a set of stone steps before arriving at a minor fork. The fork leads to a creek, which is a 30-yard walk from the trail.

The trail soon encounters another fork leading to the same creek. As the trail climbs a small hill, it passes by two wooden benches and divides. If you want to make a loop out of the hike without going to the waterfall, go right at the divide and continue on to the Children's Discovery Trail that takes you back to the trailhead. Most hikers continue on the trail that leads to the waterfall. After about 100 yards, you finally cross Lost Creek. A boulder that has fallen from above provides an arch that the trail goes under. Follow the trail to the waterfall, which is in sight from this point.

To Descend: Retrace your steps or start back on the same trail, crossing Lost Creek and heading left (west) onto the Children's Discovery Trail by the wooden benches. Follow the trail to the parking lot.

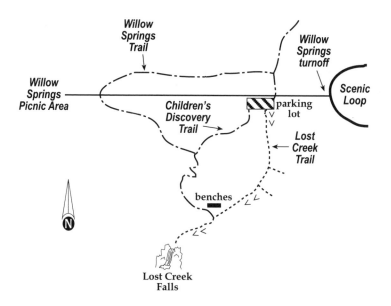

♦ ♦ ♦

Lost Creek Overlook

Hike: Lost Creek Overlook — up and back or
closed loop
Trailhead: Children's Discovery Trail — marked
Distance: 1.5 miles — one way
Elevation gain: 300 feet
Elevation peak: no peak
Time: 1 hour
Difficulty: 2
Danger level: 2
How easy to follow: 3
Children: yes
Map: La Madre Mtn., NEV

Directions: The signed turnoff for Willow Springs is located
7.3 miles past the Scenic Loop gate. Lost Creek parking area is
a fifth-of-a-mile drive from the Scenic Loop.

Overview: The **route** goes up through a break in the sandstone, then across the sandstone ledges to an overlook above
Lost Creek Waterfall. Photo 1 shows an overview.

Comments: An easy route with a big reward awaits anyone
who has a few hours and the desire to see the lower and upper
Lost Creek Waterfalls. The best chance of seeing the falls flowing is in early spring.

The Hike: The hike begins at the Children's Discovery Trail.
The trail heads west with very little elevation gain, it crosses
Red Rock Wash, and turns SE. The trail passes a roasting pit
marked by a BLM sign. The incline becomes moderate as the

Photo 1

trail heads westerly. At the sign, go right onto the Willow Springs Trail. Though the trail looks like it deadends at the boulders, go between and continue. Do not veer off onto the numerous side paths.

Looking toward the sandstone crags, a hill appears. Photo 2 shows the path you take to the crags. You'll feel the strenuous incline. Stay on the main path; do not take any of the minor side paths. At the top of the sandstone, head SE (140 degrees) toward Lost Creek.

Photo 3 shows the point where you climb up the sandstone slabs and head for the pine trees. Proceed in the same direction until the sandstone opens up into a large flat area. Go right (south) and head toward the two upper Lost Creek Waterfalls that come into view.

Once near the waterfalls, scramble onto the crag in Photo 4 and carefully walk out, veering to the right, to see the waterfall. The crag becomes very steep; do not leave children unattended.

Photo 2

To Descend: Retrace your steps back to the Children's Discovery Trail. From there, you can make a loop of the hike by going right (east) and intersecting the Lost Creek Trail. Go left (north) onto Lost Creek Trail, which is by the wooden benches. The trail leads back to the parking lot.

Photo 3

Photo 4

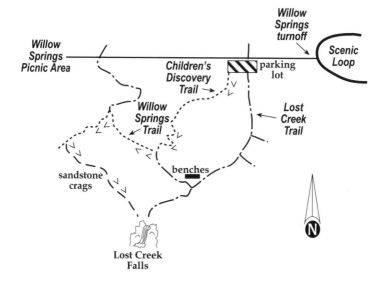

◆　◆　◆

North Peak

Hike: North Peak — up and back
Trailhead: Willow Springs Picnic Area
Distance: 8 miles — round trip
Elevation gain: 2,694 feet
Elevation peak: 7,094 feet
Time: 5 to 6 hours
Difficulty: 4
Danger level: 2
How easy to follow: 4
Children: no
Map: La Madre Mtn., NEV

Directions: The signed turnoff for Willow Springs is located 7.3 miles past the Scenic Loop gate. It's slightly more than a half-mile drive on the paved road to the gravel parking lot.

Overview: Hike the Rocky Gap Road for more than two miles, then straight up the mountain on a hard-to-follow **path**. Once at the ridgeline, the **route** approaches North Peak from the south.

Comments: North Peak is the highest peak in Red Rock. The views of Red Rock and Las Vegas from the peak are fantastic. Also, from the peak it's a half-mile hike to an awesome over-look straight down into Ice Box Canyon.

The Hike: The hike begins on the Rocky Gap Road. Walk or drive a four-wheel-drive vehicle a little more than two miles to a low spot where a gravel road comes in from the right. (See Photo 1.) At this point the hike becomes a route in search of the North Peak path that runs parallel and just below the gray ridge. Though there are many ways to find the path, the following is the recommended route. Go east (left) as indicated in Photo 1, crossing a gravel bed, descending a

Photo 1

small hill, and crossing a wide gravel wash. Just to the right (south) in the middle of the wash stands a large juniper. Follow the path, which veers slightly to the right passing a couple of boulders, and down across a second smaller wash. Follow the path up a steep hill and go right (south) onto an abandoned road at the top of the hill. You're now walking parallel to the gray ridgeline and the North Peak path. Continue about 20 yards on the abandoned dirt road and look for the faint path on the left that goes between two trees. Currently, a cairn marks the start of the path. Follow it about 20 yards where it intersects the North Peak path.

The path heads east as it climbs along the ridgeline. (See Photo 2 for an overview of the route.) If you lose the path,

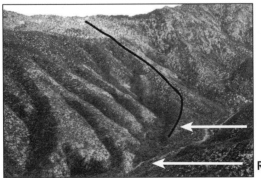

gray ridgeline

Rocky Gap Road

Photo 2

Photo 3

you've probably headed too far south (right). Hike in a northerly direction until you find it again.

The path climbs to a flat area marked by rock pinnacles. From there, it hugs the north edge of the ridgeline and becomes a strenuous hike to another flat area. The path disappears as you scramble up a rock face. It resumes, then disappears again as you scramble up another rock face (seen in Photo 3). The path becomes steep at times as it climbs switchbacks past the pinion pines and other vegetation. But it levels off before the final scramble to the ridgeline. Near the ridgeline the terrain changes to broken sandstone slabs. At this point the hike becomes very strenuous. Scramble up the sandstone at a northeasterly direction (70 degrees) to the ridgeline. At the ridgeline look for North Peak (shown in Photo 4). From this angle it's not an obvious peak.

Depending on your location on the ridgeline, North Peak will be almost a mile away. Make a wide loop around to the south face of North Peak to avoid the deep

North Peak

Photo 4

gully (invisible from here) that lies between the ridgeline and the peak. Climb up the south face of North Peak (as seen in Photo 5). A cairn marks the peak, but there is no sign-in book. For a fantastic overlook of Ice Box Canyon, come off the peak and head SE.

Photo 5

It's about a half mile to the overlook. The drop-off into Ice Box Canyon is more than 1,000 feet and you'll be standing at the top of Buffalo Wall. This is a good spot to rest and eat, since North Peak is normally very windy.

To Descend: There are a couple of options from this point. You can return the way you came up or you can hike to Bridge Mountain. If hiking to Bridge, you should have at least six hours of daylight left.

◆ ◆ ◆

Bridge Mountain

Hike: Bridge Mountain — up and back
Trailhead: Red Rock Summit via Rocky Gap Road
Distance: 7 to 16 miles — round trip (depending on your starting point)
Elevation gain: 2,000+ feet depending on starting point
Elevation peak: 6,460 feet
Time: 6 hours to all day
Difficulty: 5
Danger level: 5
How easy to follow: 3
Children: no
Map: La Madre Springs, NEV; Mountain Springs, NEV; and La Madre Mtn., NEV

Directions: From Willow Springs: The signed turnoff for Willow Springs is located 7.3 miles past the Scenic Loop gate. It's a sixth-of-a-mile drive on the paved road to the gravel parking lot. The unmarked Rocky Gap Road starts at the far end (west) of the parking lot. Follow it five miles to Red Rock Summit.

From Lovell Canyon Road: Take I-15 south to State Route 160. Turn right (west) and drive about 15 miles on 160 to Lovell Canyon Road. Turn right (north) and travel seven miles to an unsigned gravel road on the right. This is the other end of the Rocky Gap Road. Look for a "Not County Maintained Road" sign 50 yards up on the right side. Walk or drive around the bend and through a gate and continue four miles to Red Rock Summit.

Overview: Travel up Rocky Gap Road by four-wheel-drive or on foot to Red Rock Summit. The **trail** starts at the summit and proceeds east to the ridgeline. It makes a half circle south of Bridge Mountain, then the **route** heads NE across the sandstone bench to the base of Bridge Mountain. From the base, it's a series of cracks and ramps to the Natural Bridge. From the Bridge, it's up a steep ramp to the top of Bridge Mountain. The route portion of the hike is marked by black arrows and cairns.

Comments: You will remember this hike for the rest of your life! With sheer drops of 1,000 feet and Las Vegas in the background, the view has to be seen to be believed. Hikers spend hours exploring the Natural Bridge and the Hidden Forest, and admiring the view from the peak. People have come from all over the country to do this hike—they're not disappointed. Note: Wind gusts of 50 mph are common on Bridge Mountain.

The Hike: The trail starts at the summit of Rocky Gap Road. Two fence posts and three boulders mark the trailhead. (See Photo 1.) The trail starts off at a moderate grade and soon forks; take the left fork. The grade becomes steep as it heads east toward the ridgeline. When the

Photo 1

trail splits again, go left down a steep hill. Looking off to the left (west), the Rocky Gap Road is seen winding through the canyon. At about a mile, the trail reaches the ridgeline known as the "Top of the Escarpment." The trail has climbed over 700 feet.

From the Top of the Escarpment, you get your first view of Bridge Mountain. The change in the landscape from gray dolomite and trees to bare red and white sandstone is dramatic. Although it appears you could head straight toward

Bridge Mountain, you can't. Ice Box Canyon stands in your way. Turn right (south) and continue on the trail for about a mile. The trail descends about 200 feet as it heads toward the south face of Bridge Mountain. When the trail turns from gray to dark red, start looking for the cairn marking the path shown in Photo 2.

Go left (north) at the cairn and follow a faint path down the red sandstone. Look for cairns marking the way down to the white sandstone. When the ground becomes level, go right (east) 10 yards to the edge and look down. You will be looking 1,000 feet down into the north fork of Pine Creek; out to the east is Las Vegas. This is a great spot for photos. Walk back 10 yards to the west and continue toward Bridge Mountain. The route enters a wash.

The idea is to climb down the sandstone bench you are on and head toward Bridge Mountain. Do this by following cairns and two black

Photo 2

Photo 3

parallel lines, sort of ditto marks, painted on the rock (as shown in Photo 5). Take care; there are sheer drop-offs on either side. Photo 3 highlights the route.

The first part of the route to the base of Bridge Mountain descends slightly and has few cairns and markings. The idea is to keep heading toward the base of Bridge. The second part of the route descends nearly 500 feet and is well marked. There are three chutes that must be located to make this 500-foot descent. Photos 4 and 5 show the first two chutes. The third chute starts only a

Photo 4

few feet from the second chute. Cairns and the black markings lead you to the third chute. After descending the third chute, follow the cairns and black markings that lead the way to the base of Bridge Mountain.

Once at the base, follow the black markings and cairns to the correct crack. Stay in the crack until the black markings indicate a climb to the right (east). The black markings show you where to climb out of the crack and up the beehive sandstone. People who have a fear of heights should stay in the crack. The climb outside it is exposed. Staying in the crack is more protected, but it is a harder climb.

As the crack passes a ledge, the black markings lead you

Photo 5

Photo 6

left (west) on the wide ledge for about five yards. Follow the markings when they indicate to go right (north) and climb up onto a ramp. Follow the ramp to the 30-foot-tall and 50-foot-wide Natural Bridge. On the other side of the bridge, a giant ponderosa pine leans against the sandstone. This is a great area to take a break and leave the timid hikers to explore. Continue by going under the Natural Bridge and up the very steep ramp on the left wall. A huge log lies to the right of the ramp. At the top of the Natural Bridge, the domed peak of Bridge Mountain can be seen. Go SE across the sandstone rim and around the Hidden Forest.

The final ascent follows a steep ramp, which is well-marked with cairns, NE to the top. (See Photo 6.) At the top of the ramp the peak can be seen by looking to the south. It's an easy 60-yard trek to the peak from this point.

You made it! What appeared to be impossible turned out to be eminently possible when you employed the proper approach. Maybe you can apply this principle to more than climbing physical mountains. If you're standing at the peak, you've just climbed the toughest mountain of all—the one in your mind.

A large cairn with a sign-in book marks the peak. A natural shelter sits just below the peak. This is a good place to have lunch and escape the wind. The view from the peak is awesome.

To Descend: Retrace your steps down the ramp, past the Hidden Forest, and under the Natural Bridge. If you have trouble finding the Natural Bridge, look for the top of the pine that towers above the sandstone. From this point, cairns and the black markings make the descent easy to follow. Once on the trail, make sure to turn left (west) at the Top of the Escarpment. Otherwise, the trail takes you toward North Peak.

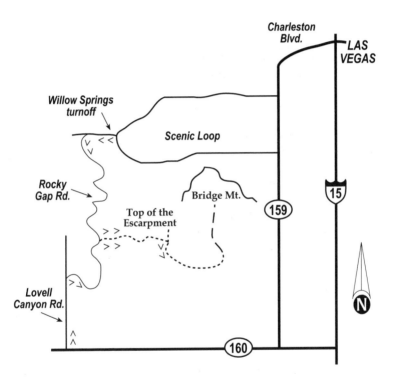

◆ ◆ ◆

Willow Springs Caves

Hike: Willow Springs Caves — up and back
Trailhead: Rocky Gap Road
Distance: 3 miles — round trip (starting at Willow Springs parking area)
Elevation gain: 400 feet
Elevation peak: 5,021 feet
Time: 1.5 hours
Difficulty: 2
Danger level: 2
How easy to follow: 4
Children: yes
Map: Blue Diamond, NEV

Directions: The signed turnoff for Willow Springs is located 7.3 miles past the Scenic Loop gate. It's slightly more than a half-mile drive on the paved road to the gravel parking lot.

Overview: The **route** starts on the Rocky Gap Road, then it's a scramble to the caves.

Comments: Being one of the shortest and safest scrambling routes in the book, this is a good hike to determine whether you like scrambling. The route goes up to the caves; however, the main cave can not be reached without ropes. You can drive on the Rocky Gap Road and park in Red Rock Wash. This cuts the distance of the hike in half.

The Hike: The hike begins at the Rocky Gap Road. Drive or walk to the turnoff for La Madre Springs Trail. Don't turn onto that trail; instead go to the small pulloff on the left (south) side of the road and follow the red dirt path that begins from the pulloff. (See Photo 1.) The path starts off steep as it heads SW up to the cave area. When it appears to deadend, climb up the white boulders, follow the path to the divide, and go left. You keep to the right side of a pinion pine before you inter-sect another path. Go left at the intersection and weave through a patch of manzanita. The path passes to the right of another pinion pine as it heads toward the sandstone. Following the footprints of other hikers be-fore you will help you stay on

Photo 1

course. The path ends at a patch of scrub oak. Make your way past the scrub oak to the white and pinkish sandstone. Climb up the sandstone as shown in Photo 2. Once at the top, go left and pick up the path. At this point the caves are visible and appear to be less than 100 yards away.

The idea is to head for the flat area of sandstone in Photo 3. From there to the top, you'll find out if you like scrambling. The path passes between a ju-niper and a pinion pine. Past the trees, the path heads SW, but this is not where you want to go. Hike left (east) across and up the sandstone as outlined in Photo 3. Once up onto this level of sandstone, look for the pin-ion pine and the boulder that appears as if it might come tumbling down. Scramble up

Photo 2

Photo 3

the sandstone (200 degrees) as outlined in Photo 4. Just beyond the pine a crack forms between two boulders. Go through the crack. At the top of the crack, go right, climbing up the sandstone to the crag. If you wind up in some bushes, you didn't turn to the right soon enough. When the crag impedes your travel, scramble along the east side of it to the 20-foot-tall pinion pine. To the right of the pine a path forms and heads west along the right (north) side of the sandstone wall to the pinion pine in Photo 5. Once at the tree, you can look to the west and see the Rocky Gap Road as it weaves up to Red Rock Summit. To the north you can see White Rock Hills Peak and most of the scrambling route that leads to the peak. It's easy scrambling up here, so you can explore some of the caves you saw from the trailhead.

To Descend: Find the pinion pine at the top and follow the path down to the second pinion pine. Go into the crack and down the sandstone. From this point, you can see the path off to the left (west) and the Rocky Gap Road.

Photo 4

Photo 5

◆ ◆ ◆

Willow Springs Loop

Hike: Willow Spring's Loop — closed loop
Trailhead: Children's Discovery Trail — marked
Distance: 1.5 miles
Elevation gain: 100 feet
Elevation peak: no peak
Time: 1 hour
Difficulty: 1
Danger level: 1
How easy to follow: 1
Children: yes
Map: La Madre Mtn., NEV

Directions: The signed turnoff for Willow Springs is located 7.3 miles past the Scenic Loop gate. Lost Creek parking area is a fifth of a mile from the turnoff.

Overview: The **trail** circles the Willow Springs Picnic Area.

Comments: The trail passes ancient Indian exhibits. BLM signs explain their significance.

The Hike: The trail begins heading west with little elevation gain. It soon crosses Red Rock Wash and turns SE, passing an ancient roasting pit marked by a BLM sign. The incline becomes moderate as the trail heads west. Go right onto the Willow Springs Trail at the sign. Two large boulders make it appear that the trail deadends; go between them and continue. Don't veer onto any of the numerous side paths. The trail makes a hard right as a path intersects from the left (south). After the intersection you get a good view of Willow Springs Picnic Area.

The trail descends rapidly and soon crosses the Red Rock Wash again. When it crosses the paved road near the picnic area, continue north passing picnic tables and barbecue pits until you pick up the trail again. As you head east, you pass two BLM signs highlighting ancient Indian artifacts. Go right at the fork; you soon cross a dry creekbed. You'll see many yuccas and beavertail cacti near the trail. At the BLM trail sign, continue on the same trail; do not go left. In about 100 yards the trail crosses the road and ends where it began.

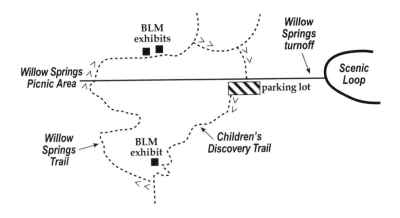

◆ ◆ ◆

La Madre Springs

Hike: La Madre Springs — up and back
Trailhead: Rocky Gap Road
Distance: 4 miles — round trip
Elevation gain: 800 feet
Elevation peak: no peak
Time: 2 hours
Difficulty: 1
Danger level: 1
How easy to follow: 1
Children: yes
Map: La Madre Mtn., NEV

Directions: The signed turnoff for Willow Springs is located 7.3 miles past the Scenic Loop gate. It's slightly more than a half-mile drive on the paved road to the gravel parking lot.

Overview: The **trail** goes up Rocky Gap Road, then north onto the signed White Rock/Willow Springs/La Madre Trail. Stay on the La Madre Trail to the springs.

Comments: La Madre Springs is a year-round water source for mule deer and bighorn sheep.

The Hike: The trail starts at the beginning of Rocky Gap Road. Follow the road for a half mile and turn right (north) onto the signed White Rock/Willow Springs/La Madre Trail. The trail heads north at a slight grade. To the east is enormous White Rock Hills Mountain. The grade increases as the trail heads NW toward the spring. Three large boulders on the right side of the trail mark the turnoff for the White Rock/Willow Springs hike. That hike goes around White Rock Hills Peak (see p. 156).

Stay on the main trail when another fork comes in on the right side. When the trail passes a large grove of junipers, look for concrete foundations. These are the remains of a cabin and archery building. The trail comes to a high point and descends 30 yards to La Madre Springs Dam. (See Photo 1.) Do not wade into the water; it's a main water source for animals in the area.

Photo 1

To Descend: Retrace your steps back to the Willow Springs parking area or follow the path that travels to the south (left) of the springs for further exploration. The path, which turns into a route, goes to La Madre Mountain.

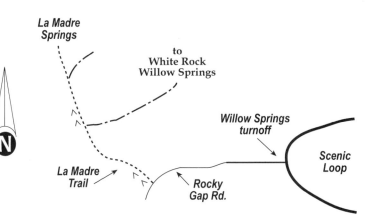

♦ ♦ ♦

Three Waterfalls

Hike: Three Waterfalls — up and back
Trailhead: Willow Springs Picnic Area
Distance: 4 miles — round trip
Elevation gain: 800 feet
Elevation peak: no peak
Time: 2.5 hours
Difficulty: 2
Danger level: 2
How easy to follow: 2
Children: yes
Map: La Madre Mtn., NEV

Directions: The signed turnoff for Willow Springs is located 7.3 miles past the Scenic Loop gate. It's slightly more than a half-mile drive on the paved road to the gravel parking lot.

Overview: The **route** follows Rock Gap Road, then heads west up the creekbed.

Comments: The hike passes two dry waterfalls and terminates at the third dry waterfall. Shortly after a rain is your best chance to see water flowing down the falls.

The Hike: The trailhead starts at the beginning of Rocky Gap Road. Follow the road for a little more than a mile. You'll pass a reddish-dirt turnaround (for cars) on the left (east) side of the road. Look for the creekbed on the right (west) side of the road. (See Photo 1.) If you pass a second reddish-dirt turnaround, you've gone about 40 yards too far. The creekbed has two brushy areas in the first 100 yards. Don't despair; after making your way past the brush, the creekbed is free of brush.

Hike west in the creekbed, past the first waterfall. Staying in the creekbed makes travel easier and faster. There are side paths in case water becomes a problem. You can climb (class II) up the left (south) side of the second waterfall unless water is flowing. A path on the right (north) side goes up and around the second waterfall. Stay on the right (north) side of the creekbed and climb up to the final waterfall. Photo 2 shows the final waterfall (dry).

Photo 1

To Descend: Retrace your steps.

Photo 2

♦ ♦ ♦

Icebox Canyon

Hike: Ice Box Canyon — up and back
Trailhead: Ice Box Canyon pulloff — marked
Distance: 2.5 miles — round trip
Elevation gain: 320 feet
Elevation peak: no peak
Time: 2 to 3 hours
Difficulty: 2
Danger level: 1
How easy to follow: 1
Children: yes
Map: Blue Diamond, NEV

Directions: The signed turnoff for Ice Box Canyon is located eight miles past the Scenic Loop gate. The pulloff is on the right side of the road, with overflow parking on the left side of the road.

Overview: This BLM **trail** goes across the desert to the mouth of the canyon, then it's a bouldering **route** to a seasonal waterfall.

Comments: This popular hike can be done in the summer months if you get an early start. Many people have tried to find routes above the waterfall, but the consensus is that ropes are needed. Be careful not to twist an ankle on the numerous rocks that lie on the trail.

The Hike: The trail heads SSW as it descends toward the Red Rock Wash. As the trail crosses the wash, instead of going directly across, it heads to the right. Rocks mark the left boundary of the trail. Flat-rock stairs help the trail climb out of the wash. Just before reaching the top of the bank, the trail goes off to the right and continues toward the mouth of the canyon. There's a slight incline as the trail passes manzanita and scrub oak. When you come to a junction, go left and continue on the rocky surface. As you go between two boulders, you get the first glimpse of the stream fed by Ice Box Canyon. In the winter months, the snowmelt from above fills the stream with rushing water. It's strange to see and hear water flowing as you walk through the middle of a desert.

The trail travels to the edge of the bank and overlooks the stream. Huge ponderosa pines stand at the edge of the stream. Numerous side paths head toward the stream; the main trail eventually takes you there too. When the trail divides, take either fork; the routes rejoin in about 75 feet. As you near the mouth of the canyon, the walls rise hundreds of feet into the air. (See Photo 1.) The walls prevent the sun from shining into the canyon, hence the name Ice Box.

Photo 1

The trail goes off to the left and descends down into the wash. It's easy to miss this turnoff. If you do, the trail ends shortly. Just retrace your steps, about 30 yards, to the turnoff, which will be on your right. Once in the wash, it's about a quarter mile of boulder hopping to reach the waterfall.

Due to the varying amounts of water in the wash, it's not possible to recommend a consistent route to the waterfall. The winter months offer the best chance of seeing water flowing; however, if the water level is high, it's impossible to reach the waterfall without getting wet.

To Descend: Retrace your steps.

♦ ♦ ♦

Pine Creek/South Fork

Hike: Pine Creek-South Fork — up and back
Trailhead: Pine Creek — marked
Distance: 4 miles — round trip
Elevation gain: none
Elevation peak: no peak
Time: 2 to 3 hours
Difficulty: 1
Danger level: 1
How easy to follow: 2
Children: yes
Map: Blue Diamond, NEV and La Madre Mtn., NEV

Directions: The signed parking area for Pine Creek Canyon is 10.3 miles past the Scenic Loop gate.

Overview: Hike down the Pine Creek **trail** to the wash that leads to a bouldering **route** in the south fork of the canyon.

Comments: This beginner's route is a good introduction to bouldering. The hike ends at a year-round pool that is an excellent place to eat lunch and relax.

The Hike: Pine Creek Trail descends in a southerly direction and soon turns to the west toward the mouth of the canyon. Looking toward the canyon, you see the ponderosa pines towering above the desert floor. It's rare to encounter these pines below 6,000 feet. The elevation along the trail is about 4,000 feet. The trail passes the turnoff for the Fire Ecology Trail, which loops back into this trail about 30 yards ahead. When the trail passes the cement foundation of the old Wilson homestead, you've hiked about eight-tenths of a mile. A photograph of the Wilson home is on display at the Visitors Center.

As you approach the mouth of Pine Creek, a huge pyramid-shaped formation called the Mescalito splits the canyon into north and south forks. The trail veers to the north as it parallels the stream that flows from the canyon. At this point, you can see all the way to the end of the north fork of Pine Creek. The top of the sheer wall at the end of the north fork is the overlook where hikers stop while hiking the Bridge Mountain route.

The trail soon crosses a dry wash and travels to the south bank of the wash. You can enter the wash at this point, but the wash soon becomes filled with water, making the hiking slow. You don't want to get wet if the water is cold, since you might be hiking in the shade later. Don't expect the water to be warm until late spring!

The trail heads south crossing another dry wash. This marks your departure from the established trail, as it turns back to the east away from the canyon. Follow the path at the bottom of the wash as it heads toward the canyon. When the path forks in 20 yards, take the right fork. The path goes between two large boulders and over an area filled with rocks before it becomes easy to follow. It weaves through the manzanita and scrub oak before crossing the wash again. Once on the north side of the wash, the path becomes easier to follow. The path has a slight incline as it heads NW and passes a tree that has died due to fire.

The paths start to spider-web in many directions, making it almost impossible to follow the same route each time. At this point, you're so close to the wash and the entrance to the canyon that your only concern is selecting the path that has the least amount of brush. No matter which path you travel, you'll soon be above the wash. Here you'll encounter more paths leading into the wash. Again, choose a path that looks free of brush. Photo 1 shows the gully that runs up the south wall of the south fork of Pine Creek. You should descend into the wash by the time you are just past even with this gully.

The amount of water and the time of year are important factors relative to the ease of travel through the wash. If it's

Photo 1

warm and the wash contains little water, you should make good time; however, if it's cold and the wash contains lots of water, travel will be slower. The beginning of the wash is free of the boulders that sometimes block progress. This part of the wash is wider than most of the washes found in the other canyons. The wash soon travels alongside the north wall of the wash. If you encounter a large pool of water, look for a path on the left that skirts the water. The wash heads SW through the canyon and is mostly a class I route. Looking up the canyon, you'll see two ponderosa pines standing guard in front of the point where the canyon divides. You soon come to a pool that's the perfect place to sit and admire the beauty of Pine Creek. Photo 2 shows the pool. A path leads around the left side of the pool. The path involves a class

Photo 2

II climb over boulders. The sure-footed can try to squeeze by the red boulder that hugs the right side of the pool. The consequence for failing is slipping into the water. The pool marks the end of the hike, as getting into the south divide beyond the ponderosa pines involves some class III moves.

To Descend: Retrace your steps.

◆ ◆ ◆

Pine Creek/
Fire Ecology Trail

Hike: Pine Creek/Fire Ecology Trail — up and back or closed loop
Trailhead: Pine Creek — marked
Distance: 1 mile — round trip
Elevation gain: none
Elevation peak: no peak
Time: 30 minutes
Difficulty: 1
Danger level: 1
How easy to follow: 1
Children: yes
Map: Blue Diamond, NEV and La Madre Mtn., NEV

Directions: The signed parking area for Pine Creek Canyon is 10.3 miles past the Scenic Loop gate.

Overview: You stroll down the BLM-maintained Pine Creek **trail** and onto the Fire Ecology Loop **trail**.

Comments: A perfect hike for those interested in how the BLM uses controlled burning to manage the growth of vegetation. The trail has a couple of benches to watch the water in Pine Creek.

The Hike: Pine Creek Trail descends south and soon turns west toward the mouth of the canyon. Looking toward the canyon, you see the ponderosa pines towering above the desert floor; it's rare to encounter these pines below 6,000 feet (the elevation along the trail is about 4,000 feet). Turn left onto the Fire Ecology Trail. The trail remains flat as it heads south, passing juniper, yucca, and scrub oak. After descending a couple of steps, the trail turns west and parallels a dry creekbed.

Go left (south) onto the trail that crosses the wooden bridge. A picnic table lies off to the right. Follow the left loop of the trail as it heads toward a year-round stream (Pine Creek). You can sit on the benches and watch the water flow. A number of nearby BLM signs explain the concept of controlled burning. Continue on the trail until it loops back into itself. Take the wooden bridge back to the first loop of the Fire Ecology Trail. To make a complete loop, go left; when it connects with the Pine Creek Trail, turn right and follow it to the parking lot.

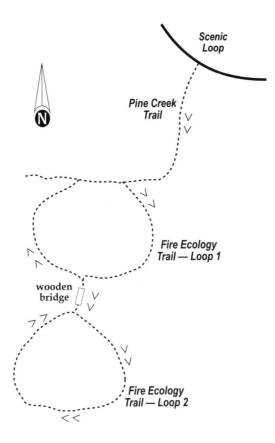

♦ ♦ ♦

Fern Canyon

Hike: Fern Canyon (north fork of Pine Creek) — up and back
Trailhead: Pine Creek — marked
Distance: 3 or 6 miles — round trip
Elevation gain: > 350 feet, > 500 feet
Elevation peak: no peak
Time: 1.5 or 3 hours
Difficulty: 1 - 2
Danger level: 1 - 2
How easy to follow: 1 - 2
Children: yes - no
Map: Blue Diamond, NEV and Mountain Springs, NEV

Directions: The signed parking area for Pine Creek Canyon is 10.3 miles past the Scenic Loop gate.

Overview: A **trail** leads into the north wash of Pine Creek. Once in the wash it's a bouldering **route.**

Comments: The hike has two stopping points. The first ends at a pool with plenty of spots for beginners or families to sit and enjoy the beauty of Fern Canyon. The second ends at a seasonal waterfall located deep within Pine Creek Canyon. For those who do not want to boulder hop, side paths along the upper right (north) bank follow the creekbed most of the way.

The Hike: Pine Creek Trail descends in a southerly direction and soon turns west toward the mouth of the canyon. Looking at the canyon, you see ponderosa pines (rare below 6,000

Photo 1

feet) towering above the desert floor. The elevation along the trail is about 4,000 feet. The trail passes the turnoff for the Fire Ecology Trail, which loops back into this trail about 30 yards ahead. Photo 1 shows the trail heading toward the canyon. When it passes the concrete foundation of the old Wilson home-

stead, you've hiked about four-fifths of a mile. A photograph of the Wilson home is on display at the Visitors Center.

As you approach the mouth of Pine Creek, a huge pyramid-shaped formation called the "Mescalito" splits the canyon into north and south forks. The main trail descends to the left (south); continue over the rock pile and onto a different trail that leads to the mouth of the North Fork. (See Photo 2.)

The trail heads SW toward the mouth of the North Fork.

Photo 2

When you come to an opening, you'll encounter three paths taking off toward the creekbed that lies at the mouth of the canyon. All the paths eventually lead into the creekbed. I recommend the following. At the three-way divide, take the path that goes straight. It weaves through scrub oak and turns right. Rocks are embedded in the path as it passes below a band of small red sandstone cliffs. The path then weaves to the north side of the creekbed and divides in another 40 yards. Take the left divide (lower path) as it descends toward the creekbed. At this point you can go into the creekbed, but it's better to stay up on the path and wait for a second path that descends brush-free into the creekbed. This path enters the creekbed 40 to 50 yards in front of a large still-standing dead tree.

The creekbed is a mixture of class I and easy class II bouldering as it heads SW. Depending on the amount of water and its temperature, the entire hike might be class I. For those who don't want to boulder hop, a path parallels the creekbed on the right (north) bank of the canyon. Just after you pass under a limb, a new path starts just feet away from the creekbed. Follow this until just after you have to step up onto a half-buried boulder. A large rock slab marks a path that leads to the right, going up and around the creekbed. The path climbs up the bank about 30 feet, then makes a hard left crossing over rocks and a boulder area. It then descends back into the creekbed. Use the path if there's too much water in the creekbed.

Follow a path that lies alongside the creekbed or boulder hop to the pool seen in Photo 3. The pool lies in the center of what local hikers have named Fern Canyon. The canyon gets its name from the ferns that grow out

Photo 3

of the rocky banks along the creekbed. It offers year-round water, plenty of places to sit, and a chance to relax in the peaceful setting. This marks the end of the short hike.

To continue, follow the creekbed up 30 to 40 yards and follow a path on the left (south) bank that weaves under the overhanging rocks. Once you reach the boulders, climb over them toward the center of the creekbed to a sandy area. Continue paralleling the creekbed as you climb up and over the boulders to the major obstacle in Photo 4. About 25 yards before the blockage near a large ponderosa pine, boulders hide a path that comes in from the right (north) side; climb up the boulders and onto the path. You head west, go through a small opening in the brush, and climb to a boulder area. Once on top of the tan-streaked boulders, you'll see the path descending into the creekbed.

Photo 4

The next part of the creekbed is absent of water and involves a few sections of class II and easy class III climbing. The creekbed changes into a wash. Your next obstacle involves a tricky climb up onto a ledge. If you miss, you'll fall into the water. Don't try this if the water is cold. Instead, walk alongside the right edge of the boulder shown in Photo 5 and climb up through the brush (not shown). This brush passage takes you around the boulder and back into the creekbed, which turns into a wash (dry).

The right (north) bank of the wash opens up, allowing you to climb onto the slanted ramps. It's best to stay in the wash for about 40 yards, till you reach an obvious walk-up to the ramps. Follow the ramps to the seasonal (winter and early

spring) 30-foot waterfall shown in Photo 6. This area also offers plenty of places to sit and relax before returning to the
trailhead.

To Descend: Retrace your steps.

Photo 5

Photo 6

♦ ♦ ♦

Juniper Canyon to Rainbow Wall

Hike: Juniper Canyon to the base of Rainbow Wall —
up and back
Trailhead: Pine Creek Canyon — marked
Distance: 8 miles — round trip
Elevation gain: 1,600 feet
Elevation peak: no peak
Time: 4 to 5 hours
Difficulty: 3
Danger level: 2
How easy to follow: 3
Children: no
Map: Blue Diamond, NEV

Directions: The signed parking area for Pine Creek Canyon
is 10.3 miles past the Scenic Loop gate.

Overview: Follow the Pine Creek **trail** to the Juniper **path** that
goes to the mouth of the canyon. It's a half bouldering **route**
and a half **path** through the canyon to the base of Rainbow
Wall.

Comments: This is a great hike with some unbelievable views.
Deep inside Juniper Canyon to the south lies the 1,200-foot
Rainbow Wall. To the north sits the 600-foot Brownstone Wall.
If you look hard, you might see climbers hundreds of feet up
on the walls. If you want to try the Rainbow Wall hike, do this
hike first to get an appreciation for Rainbow Wall. This is a

good test hike to see how you will fare on the longer canyon hikes. If this hike is even slightly difficult for you, do not attempt the Indecision, Mt. Wilson, or Rainbow Wall hikes. Because of brush, wear long pants and bring a long-sleeve shirt.

The Hike: The Pine Creek Trail descends in a southerly direction and soon turns west toward the mouth of the canyon. The trail passes the turnoff for the Fire Ecology Trail, which loops back into this trail about 30 yards ahead. After passing the concrete foundation for the old Wilson homestead, head 50 yards southwest down into a flat area and pick up the trail that heads toward the mouth of Pine Canyon. The trail crosses the creek in a few yards. About 50 yards after the creek crossing, Juniper path comes in from the left (south). It starts off heading south, then turns easterly as it climbs a ridge. When it divides,

take the right fork. As the path heads toward the mouth of Juniper Canyon, numerous side paths veer toward the mountain; stay on the main path. The path eventually descends into the wash that goes through the middle of Juniper Canyon. Go right (west) into the wash. Almost immediately, you're challenged by a huge

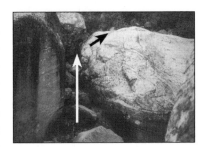

Photo 1

boulder. Climb up the left side of the boulder as shown in Photo 1.

If the boulder presents too much of a challenge, there's an alternate route. Head east instead of west when the path empties into the wash. Hike about 30 yards to a huge log that lies across the wash. Just before the log on the south bank are purplish-black boulders. Scramble up the boulders heading west past the huge boulder and drop back into the wash.

When huge boulders divide the wash, take the right (north) fork that travels alongside the right (north) wall of the canyon. As the wash heads to the center of the canyon, look for cairns that guide you through the center of the wash, which is filled with scrub oak. The wash divides near a large pinion pine; take the left fork and follow the cairns as you climb over the boulders. About 50 yards past the pinion pine, climb out of the wash and onto a path that comes in on the right (west). Notice the pine in Photo 2.

Photo 2

The path is steep but easy to follow as it heads west toward Brownstone Wall. Once the red dirt path climbs to level ground, it passes by a fallen log, then descends slightly and goes to the left of a large ponderosa pine. A two-foot-high boulder with a cairn on it marks the fork. (See Photo 3.)

The right fork leads to Brownstone Wall, the left fork to Rainbow Wall. Go onto the left path, which periodically travels alongside the left (south) wall of the canyon. When the path crosses a small boulder field, look for the cairn on the far side that marks the continuation of the route. (See Photo 4.) Go through the opening in

Photo 3

the manzanita and drop down into another wash. This wash passes to the left of the white sandstone crag as it heads toward Rainbow Wall. Photo 5 shows the class III climb up the boulders that block the wash.

About 75 yards past the class III climb, the wash becomes

very brushy. Go onto the path that comes in from the right side of the wash, then goes around the brush and drops back down into the wash. From this point Rainbow Wall is visible. Continue up the wash to the seasonal waterfall. Photo 6 shows the waterfall and the awesome Rainbow Wall. If you're fascinated with the wall, I suggest your next hike be to the top of the wall (see p. 219). A rope hangs down the center of the water-fall. I strongly advise against using the rope to climb up the waterfall. The rope has been exposed to the elements for an undetermined length of time and might not be safe. This is a perfect place to have lunch and look for climbers on the walls.

Photo 4

To Descend: Retrace your steps.

Photo 5

Photo 6

◆ ◆ ◆

Juniper Peak &
Brownstone Wall

Hike: Juniper Peak and Brownstone Wall — up and back
Trailhead: Pine Creek Canyon — marked
Distance: 10 miles — round trip
Elevation gain: 2,109 feet
Elevation peak: 6,109 feet
Time: 6 to 7 hours
Difficulty: 4
Danger level: 3
How easy to follow: 4
Children: no
Map: Blue Diamond, NEV

Directions: The signed parking area for Pine Creek Canyon is 10.3 miles past the Scenic Loop gate.

Overview: Follow Pine Creek **trail** to Juniper **path**. A half bouldering **route** and half **path** leads through the canyon. Then it's a scrambling **route** to Juniper Peak and on to Brownstone Wall Overlook.

Comments: This hike has plenty to offer: a trail to warm up on, bouldering through a magnificent canyon, and class II scrambling. With great views of Rainbow Wall and Brownstone Wall, and an awesome overlook into the south fork of Pine Creek, this hike is one of the best in the book.

The Hike: The Pine Creek Trail descends in a southerly direction and soon turns west toward the mouth of the canyon. The trail passes the turnoff for the Fire Ecology Trail. When the trail passes the concrete foundation for the old Wilson homestead, hike 50 yards southwest down into a flat grassy area and pick up the obvious trail that heads to the mouth of the canyon. The trail crosses the creek in a few yards. About 50 yards farther, Juniper Path comes in from the left (south). It starts off heading south, then turns easterly as it climbs a ridge. When it divides, take the right fork. As it heads toward the mouth of Juniper Canyon, numerous side paths veer toward the mountain; stay on the main path. The path eventually descends into the wash that goes up the middle of Juniper Canyon. Go right (west) into the wash. Almost immediately, you're challenged by a huge boulder. Climb up the left side of the boulder as shown in Photo 1 of the Juniper to Rainbow Wall hike (see p. 206).

If the boulder presents too much of a challenge, an alternate route exists. Head east instead of west when the path empties into the wash. Hike about 30 yards to a huge log that lies across the wash. Look for the purplish-black boulders on the south bank a few feet before the log. Climb up the boulders, head west, and drop back into the wash.

When huge boulders divide the wash, take the right (north) fork that travels next to the right (north) wall of the canyon. As you head to the center of the canyon, look for cairns that guide you through the center of the wash. The wash divides near a large pinion pine; take the left fork and follow the cairns as you climb over the boulders. About 50 yards past the pinion pine, climb out of the wash and onto a path that comes in on the right (west). See Photo 2 in the Juniper Canyon to Rainbow Wall hike. (See p. 207.)

The path is steep but easy to follow as it heads west toward Brownstone Wall. Once the red dirt path climbs to level ground, it passes a fallen log, then descends slightly and goes left of a large ponderosa pine. A two-foot-high boulder with a cairn on it marks the point where the path divides; the right fork leads to Juniper Peak, the left to Rainbow Wall. See Photo 3 in the Juniper Canyon to Rainbow Wall hike.

Take the right fork and immediately climb over boulders as the path veers slightly left before dropping into another wash. At the wash go left and boulder through for about 50 yards. On the right side is an opening in the brush—keep a sharp eye out; it's easy to miss. The hiker in Photo 1 stands next to the opening. Notice the ponderosa pine in the background.

Hike up the steep path through the brush and over boulders. The path empties into a boulder field. Head SW

Photo 1

(240 degrees) through the boulder field, looking for a large black boulder with a cairn on top. Just to the right and a little beyond the black boulder, the path resumes. It cuts through the brush and empties out at the white sandstone. The towering reddish-brown wall ahead is Brownstone Wall.

Photo 2

Scramble NW to the boulder circled in Photo 2. Use the pinnacle on the ridgeline in Photo 2 as a landmark, but don't scramble all the way to the base of Brownstone Wall. Once at the boulder, go NE toward the red boulders in Photo 3. Hike up the drainage filled with rocks just behind the

first red boulder. (See Photo
4.) The drainage empties out
onto the white, steep, slanted
sandstone. It's easier to go
around to the right of the red
boulder to get past the initial
steep section of the white
sandstone. Your goal is to get
into the chute that leads to the
top. Photo 5 shows the turtle-
shaped boulder that over-
looks the chute. Keep this in
sight as you make your way
north toward the chute.

Photo 3

Once on the white sand-
stone, head toward the juniper that sits at the top of this
strenuous trek. Follow the
faint path that starts just left of the juniper. The steep path
veers right before emptying onto another section of white sandstone. A dead tree lies at the top of the sandstone. The next

path is just beyond the dead
tree. Follow as it weaves
through the manzanita, to
the left of a large boulder,
and ends at a juniper. Just
behind the juniper is a low
point in the sandstone wall.
Climb up the sandstone and
toward the chute in Photo 6.
Stay to the right side of the
chute, then run up the steep
wall to the pinion pine.

From the pinion pine,
head west up the beehive
sandstone to the passage that
leads to the top. Photo 7
shows the start of the passage. Stay to the right of the

Photo 4

Photo 5

pinkish boulder in Photo 7 and follow the path that hugs the left (south) wall. This is a strenuous class II climb.

At the top of the passage, go right to a fantastic overlook of the south fork of Pine Creek. After taking in the view, head left just past the second of three large ponderosa pines. Go left (east) onto the boulders and slabs, but stay near the wall. Climb off the last boulder into the chute in Photo 8. Go under the boulder, then climb through the hole and out onto the sandstone. Head toward the large pinion that stands at the top of the sandstone. Turn left (SE) and go between the sandstone mounds to the top. Look for the cairn that marks Juniper Peak.

From here you can descend or travel another half mile to an awesome overlook straight down Brownstone Wall. If you go on to the overlook, head SSW (210 degrees) along the top of Brownstone Wall. It's an easy class I and II hike to the overlook. Go to the slanted section just before the greenish wall that marks the end of the hike. Look over the edge of Brownstone Wall carefully. (See Photo 9.)

To Descend: Retrace your steps.

Photo 6

Photo 7

Photo 8

Photo 9

◆ ◆ ◆

Oak Creek

Hike: Oak Creek Canyon — up and back
Trailhead: Oak Creek Canyon turnoff — marked
Distance: 3 miles — round trip
Elevation gain: 200 feet
Elevation peak: no peak
Time: 2 hours
Difficulty: 2
Danger level: 2
How easy to follow: 2
Children: Yes
Map: Blue Diamond, NEV

Directions: The signed turnoff road for Oak Creek Canyon is located a little more than 12 miles past the Scenic Loop gate. Turn right on the gravel road and drive three-quarters of a mile to the trailhead.

Overview: The BLM **trail** heads to the mouth of the canyon, where it drops down into a wash. From there it's a bouldering **route** through the canyon.

Comments: This is a classic bouldering route that includes many options for further exploration. A route leads to Mt. Wilson via Oak Creek Canyon, but I have not tried this yet. It would be an interesting hike.

The Hike: The trail starts off SW as it heads toward the mouth of Oak Creek Canyon, which lies between Mt. Wilson on the south and Rainbow Peak on the north. Rocks littering the trail make travel more difficult than it appears, since there is no incline at this point. Photo 1 shows the trail heading toward Oak Creek Canyon. As the trail draws closer to the mouth, off to the left (south) is a hill called "Wilson Pimple" or "Potato Knob." There's a slight incline at this point. Looking into

Photo 1

the canyon, it appears that 100-foot sandstone walls block the canyon shortly after entering. Looks can be deceiving.

The trail empties into the wash near a huge 15-foot boulder that rests to the left of the trail and on the north side of the wash. Take a good look at this boulder; it marks the start of the trail on your way back. The wash, filled with car-sized boulders and lined with gravel, heads SW into the canyon. Unlike First Creek, it's free of brush. About 75 yards into the wash, you dip under a large log that has fallen across two boulders. The wash soon divides; take the left (north) fork. When the wash becomes blocked by brush, go to the left through an opening in the brush. When the wash divides again, go into the left (south) fork and almost immediately cross back into the right

fork to avoid an apartment-sized boulder. When you encounter a blockage due to boulders, you can climb over them (class III) or follow the path that goes around them to the left. The wash turns to the north temporarily and heads toward Rain-

Photo 2

bow Peak before turning back to the south. Southbound, the red dirt and bluffs at the north base of Mt. Wilson come into view. Photo 2 reveals another blockage. This can be avoided by taking a side path that goes around the left side of the boulders. So far the wash has been dry, but this will change if hiking in the early spring.

Up on the right (north) side, you'll notice a black-colored, bowl-shaped formation in the side of the canyon wall. It's called the "Lower Painted

Photo 3

Bowl." This part of the wash is marked by car-sized boulders. When the wash forks, go into the right fork. Soon you'll encounter a section of class III climbing to get on top of a boulder. Photo 3 shows the boulder you'll need to climb to get above

Boulder

this obstacle. Children can be lifted to the top of the boulder. Photo 4 shows the triangular-shaped boulder that sits in the water and marks the perfect place to stop, eat lunch, and admire the beauty of Oak Creek Canyon.

Photo 4

To Descend: Retrace your steps, looking for the boulder that marks the start of the trail.

◆ ◆ ◆

Rainbow Wall

Hike: Rainbow Wall — up and back
Trailhead: Oak Creek pulloff
Distance: 14 miles — round trip
Elevation gain: 3,072 feet
Elevation peak: 6,924 feet
Time: 8 to 10 hours
Difficulty: 5
Danger level: 5
How easy to follow: 5
Children: No
Map: Blue Diamond, NEV and Mountain Springs, NEV

Directions: The signed turnoff road for Oak Creek Canyon is located a little more than 12 miles past the Scenic Loop gate. Turn right on the gravel road and drive three-quarters of a mile to the trailhead. (The alternate trailhead is located on State Route 159, 3.5 miles past the turnoff for Red Rock, but this adds another two miles of hiking, round trip, to an already long hike.)

Overview: Follow the **trail** into the canyon, go right when the canyon divides, and go right at the final fork. Once out of the canyon, it's a half **route**-half **path** and a strenuous class I trek to Rainbow Wall.

Comments: Imagine looking 1,200 feet straight down. That's exactly what you do once you hike to the very edge of Rainbow Wall. Climbers from around the country come to climb Rainbow Wall. We are using their descent route as our hike to the top of Rainbow Wall. This is one of the hardest and most rewarding hikes in the book. Do not attempt this hike unless you are very comfortable on class III rock and are in very good shape. The best time to do this hike is mid-spring, before it gets too hot.

The Hike: The trail heads SW toward the mouth of Oak Creek Canyon. The canyon lies between Mt. Wilson to the south and Rainbow Peak to the north. As the trail draws closer to the mouth, off to the left (south) is a hill called the "Wilson Pimple" or "Potato Knob." The incline becomes slight at this point. The trail empties into the wash by a huge 15-foot boulder that rests to the left of the trail and lies on the north side of the wash. Take a good look at this boulder; it marks the start of the trail on your way back. The wash heads SW into the canyon. It's filled with car-sized boulders and lined with gravel. About 75 yards into the wash, you dip under a large log. The wash soon divides; take the left (south) fork. When brush blocks the wash, go to the left through an opening in the brush. The wash divides again; go into the left (south) fork and almost immediately cross back into the right fork to avoid an apartment-sized boulder. When you encounter a blockage due to boulders, you can climb over the boulders (class III) or follow the path to the left that goes around them. The wash turns to the north temporarily and heads toward Rainbow Peak before turning back to the south. As the wash heads south, it travels toward the red dirt and red bluffs at the north base of Mt. Wilson.

Up on the right (north) side you'll notice a black bowl-shaped formation in the side of the canyon wall called the "Lower Painted Bowl." This part of the wash is marked by car-sized boulders. When the wash forks, take the right fork. Soon you'll encounter a section of class III climbing to get on top of a boulder. Hike to the triangular-shaped boulder that sits in the water. (See Photo 1 in the Oak Creek Canyon hike, p. 217.) A path leads around the water on the left (south) side. Continue up the wash to where the canyon divides. (See Photo 1.) Take the right (north) fork as it heads west into the canyon. Soon after entering this fork, you come across a major blockage. Look for the steep slanted boulder to the right that has a

Photo 1

pile of rocks at its base. Climb up the boulder and continue bouldering through this mostly class II section of the canyon. Small cairns strategically placed assure you that someone has been here before.

Generally, the default is to the right of huge boulders that block the middle of the wash. Depending on snowmelt and rainfall, you might encounter water near the point where the right (east) bank becomes slanted slabs of sandstone. A path on the right (east) side of the canyon can be hiked for about 75 yards to avoid the water and the brush. The path drops back into the wash and the bouldering becomes mostly class II.

When two huge ponderosa pines come into view, a path forms on the left side of the wash, which avoids the water and brush. This path eventually leads you back into the wash. The wash forks; take the left fork, which is free of water and brush. At this point a huge sandstone formation with an overhang sits high on the left side of the canyon. A path on the right side of the wash avoids the water and the multiple waterfalls. This path takes you to the slanted east bank in Photo 2.

Photo 2

Notice the two ponderosa pines in the background.

Soon you'll come to a steep slanted section of sandstone with a waterfall trickling down the center. About halfway up, the slanted sandstone becomes very slick. It's best to avoid this area by climbing about 30 yards up the steep slabs located on the right (east) bank. Look for a "suzan" (see Glossary for the definition) and a large overhanging boulder that sits in the brush to the left of the sandstone slabs. A faint path cuts through the brush and leads to the top of the waterfall. The first ponderosa pine now lies about 50 yards ahead of you. Hike past the first ponderosa pine to your right. Look for a path that takes you to the second ponderosa pine. Continue up the canyon.

At this point a decision to stay in the wash or climb up the east bank needs to be made. If too much water is in the wash or the grapevines are alive, you need to make the traverse along the upper east bank. If water and brush are not a problem, stay in the wash and continue bouldering.

If you make the east-bank traverse, find the gutter that leads up the right (east) bank. Once up the gutter, climb up the very slanted sandstone slabs to a point where the sandstone levels out. Look for small cairns marking the route. The trick is to climb all the way up to the flat area before you traverse across. If you try to traverse at a lower spot, you'll get into some very dangerous areas. Photo 3 was taken from along the traverse. Notice how the canyon bends to the left. Follow the cairns and continue the traverse until you can safely descend back into the wash near a steep slanted waterfall. You are now past the brush and

Photo 3

the route becomes a class II hike as the wash heads west up the canyon. The canyon's true beauty is revealed here. Magnificent colors and stunning formations present themselves in this last leg of the canyon. As you look up the canyon, you can see the

Photo 4

limestone cliffs marking the end of the canyon. To the right (north), Rainbow Mountain slants downward to meet up with the canyon. Make your way up to the bowl-like formation where water might be running down the center. (See Photo 4.) Getting above this bowl requires friction climbing. Stay near the center for the last 30 feet, but avoid the slippery gray and black streaks. Once above the bowl, the wash forks.

At this point you have two options. Climb up the steep sandstone slabs at the start of the right fork or continue up the right fork through the brush to the end of the wash as seen in Photo 5. It's about 200 yards from the junction to the end of the wash. Climbing up the steep sandstone slab is shorter, but it may be too much for those who did not enjoy the earlier traverse. The climb from the end of the wash goes across broken sandstone rock at a lesser incline.

If you choose to scramble up the steep sandstone slabs, head NE (320 degrees) up the sandstone. By veering to the right near the manzanita, you avoid some of the steep slabs in the beginning, but eventually you will climb up the ramp-like slabs. When the terrain flattens, go to the left of the black-faced crag in Photo 6. Climb up the

Photo 5

Photo 6

steep slabs and into the broken-chip sandstone. To the right is an unbelievable overlook of Oak Creek Canyon. Take a moment to catch your breath and admire the view.

Looking to the north, the red sandstone domes come into view. Hike toward the domes, staying beneath the craggy pinnacles on the ridge. Eventually you'll pick up a path that leads to the base of a red sandstone ramp that goes to a saddle. Aim for the tree which sits at the top of the red sandstone ramp. (See Photo 7.) It's a strenuous class I trek to the saddle.

If you choose to hike to the end of the wash in Photo 5, hike up the white sandstone chips north toward the craggy pinnacles. Pick up the path that leads to the same red sandstone ramp that goes to the saddle in Photo 7. This route misses the fantastic overlook.

From the saddle, head to the left of the red sandstone crags. (See Photo 8.) A path starts after the sandstone boulders, heads north around the large sandstone crag, and up to

Photo 7

Photo 8

the ridge. The path travels just below the sandstone crag in Photo 9.

The path climbs to the other side (south) of the ridge, goes past manzanita bushes, and ends where the sandstone starts. As you continue hiking in a northerly direction, Las Vegas comes into view. Off to your right lies the false peak of Rainbow Mountain, and behind it the real Rainbow Peak. The climb to the real Rainbow Peak requires rope, so this hike does not travel there. Rainbow Wall is more impressive and appears to be higher than the peak. Soon after you see Vegas, you'll notice that the red sandstone

Photo 9

mountain you are on turns to white sandstone up ahead. This marks the backside of Rainbow Wall. Photo 10 shows the back of Rainbow Wall. Notice the cave in Photo 10. Climb down the red sandstone (class II) onto the white sandstone. Walk up the white sandstone to the edge of Rainbow Wall.

Congratulations, you made it! It was a tough hike. Take time to appreciate the view from here. Peer straight down 1,200 feet to the base of Rainbow Wall and into Juniper Canyon. It's more than 2,500 feet down to the desert floor. The dark red wall across Juniper Canyon is Brownstone Wall. To the east lies Las Vegas; to the west the sandstone world of Red Rock. Quite a contrast in more ways than one.

To Descend: Retrace your steps.

Photo 10

◆ ◆ ◆

First Creek Waterfall

Hike: First Creek Waterfall — up and back
Trailhead: First Creek pulloff — marked
Distance: 2 miles — round trip
Elevation gain: less than 100 feet
Elevation peak: no peak
Time: less than 1 hour
Difficulty: 1
Danger level: 1
How easy to follow: 1
Children: yes
Map: Blue Diamond, NEV

Directions: Drive west on Charleston past Red Rock Canyon. Stay on Route 159 (Charleston) for five miles past the turnoff for Red Rock Canyon. Park at the signed First Creek parking area on the right (west) side of the road.

Overview: Follow the **trail** through the desert to a waterfall.

Comments: It's an amazing feeling to walk through the desert and find a hidden waterfall a few feet from the trail.

The Hike: The trail immediately crosses a dry wash as it heads SSW toward the mouth of First Creek Canyon. When the trail divides, take the left (south) fork. In a couple hundred yards, a horse path splits off to the right, avoiding the rocks that lie in the main trail. The horse path rejoins the main trail after about 10 yards. Once you're past this spot, it's about 75 yards to the path that leads to the waterfall. This path is easily missed. It veers off the main trail from the right (north) and heads NW

(310 degrees) directly toward Rainbow Peak, which is the sandstone mountain to the right (north) of Mt. Wilson. (See Photo 1.)

Photo 1

Follow this path until it leads to the edge of the creekbed. Look for the brownish boulders that lie on the far side of the bank. They're circled in Photo 1. The waterfall is in the middle of the creekbed and below the boulders. It's hard to see from the path until you're almost on top of it. If you hear the water flowing, let your ears guide you. There are plenty of places to sit, take in the beauty of the waterfall, and relax. Close your eyes and listen—really listen. Do you feel relaxed? This kind of therapy doesn't cost a thing!

To Descend: Retrace your steps.

♦ ♦ ♦

Mt. Wilson

Hike: Mt. Wilson — up and back
Trailhead: First Creek — marked
Distance: 12 miles — round trip
Elevation gain: 3,420 feet
Elevation peak: 7,070 feet
Time: 10 to 12 hours
Difficulty: 5
Danger level: 3
How easy to follow: 5
Children: no
Map: Blue Diamond, NEV

Directions: Drive west on Charleston (Route 159) past Red Rock Canyon. Stay on 159 for five miles past the turnoff to Red Rock Canyon. Park at the signed First Creek parking area on the right (west) side of the road.

Overview: The **route** goes up the creekbed, follows the north fork, then it's a long scramble to the peak.

Comments: This is one of the most difficult hikes in the book. First Creek seems endless, but the views from Mt. Wilson are the most dramatic in Red Rock. There is no "correct" route up First Creek. I've given directions around, over, and under the house-sized boulders when they seem to block the continuation of the hike. Depending on the time of year, amount of water encountered, your climbing ability, and the grapevines, you might find better routes around the boulders. Once out of the canyon, the scramble to the top seems easy. This hike should be attempted during the spring, before the grapevines come back to life. Get a very early start; you don't want to be coming back in the dark.

The Hike: The trail immediately crosses a dry wash as it heads SSW toward the mouth of First Creek Canyon. When it divides, take the left (south) fork. The trail goes down a hill as numerous side paths veer off from both sides. It passes under the branch of a 20-foot scrub oak, then parallels a stream that emanates from First Creek. This marks the end of the BLM-maintained trail. When the trail divides, go onto the fork that veers slightly right. Just before the trail heads down into the stream, two side paths come in from the left (west) and soon merge with a trail, which is easier to follow; it eventually deteriorates into a path as it stays up on the left (south) bank of the creekbed. The path comes to a high point and offers a good view of First Creek. Photo 1 was taken from this point.

Photo 1

When the path divides, take the left fork. Soon, the path descends a hill. A tree has fallen across the path near the bottom of the hill. At this point you can descend into the creekbed; however, it's quicker to follow the path as it parallels the creekbed. Also, you might encounter too much water and have to climb out of the creekbed and back onto the path. The trick is to avoid ascending too high on the south bank where numerous paths spiderweb in several directions. Look for a huge white boulder with brownish knobs on it. Just before this boulder, follow the path that veers up and to the left of the boulder. The path goes to the top of a wall of grayish white rock. Traverse the top of the grayish white rock as the path heads toward the mouth of the canyon. The path becomes easier to follow as it goes across the red sandstone and dirt. About 15 feet after the path changes from red to light brown, a minor

Photo 2

side path comes in from the right and descends into the creekbed. Look for a band of red sandstone that sits across on the north side of the canyon. A hill with boulders is to the right of the band. (See Photo 2.) The path descends due north, weaves between two boulders, and runs across small boulders as it enters the creekbed.

Once you've dropped into the creekbed, climb up the boulder to the right of the pinkish-striped boulder, and past the dead tree. The next part of the wash is normally dry and heads toward the red sandstone wall of the north side of the canyon. Some class III climbing is required to get around or over the boulders.

Photo 3 shows where this part of the wash deadends.

It's best to climb up the boulders on the left (class III) and head into the center of the canyon. Walk about 40 yards SW (240 degrees) and drop into a differ-

Photo 3

ent part of the wash. Head west in the wash until you come upon two 30-foot boulders. Find the path that weaves around the left side of the left boulder; follow it and climb on top of the boulder. In about 40 yards another blockage occurs. Photo 4 shows the class III climb to the left of the boulders blocking the wash.

When you come to a candy-striped boulder, climb the boulder that sits to the left of it and under the branches of the scrub oak. Next, a large pinkish boulder blocks your travel as you enter a bowl-like formation. Look for a patch of beavertail cacti about 15 feet up on the right (north) wall. Climb alongside the left side of the pinkish boulder and follow the path that heads up the left (south) bank. (See Photo 5.) Notice the rock tower in the background.

Photo 4

The steep path levels off as it crosses a small boulder field. Up ahead about 200 yards, you'll see a steep section of slanted red sandstone that forms the south wall of the canyon. The path resumes on the far side of the boulder field. Once the path passes above a large pinion pine, start looking for an obvious path that heads down toward a huge reddish boulder. Follow the path as it weaves between the reddish boulder and another smaller boulder. You're now in the creekbed again. You could have descended earlier, but staying on the path allowed you to bypass some major obstacles. The dry wash makes hiking easy in this part of the canyon. Photo 6 shows the boulders and the log you climb over.

Photo 5

Photo 6

Up ahead, the wash divides twice: on both occasions hike into the left fork. The wash travels along the left (south) wall of the canyon until you come to the spot in Photo 7. At this point you need to make a decision. You can follow the path in Photo 7, avoiding a tricky traverse and a class III chimney, or you can do the traverse and climb the chimney. The path is steep but safe; the climb is much quicker and more fun. If you follow the path, drop back into the wash as soon as possible and look for a 100-foot tree that has fallen into the wash. The wash divides just beyond the tree. It's important for you to drop back into the wash before it divides in order to keep track of where you are.

If you choose to do the traverse and chimney, have the best hiker in your group go first and help the others. The traverse is about 20 yards past the boulder in Photo 7. Scooting around the protruding boulder is tricky due to limited handholds. Keep walking to the apparent dead-end of the wash. Photo 8 shows a hiker standing at the entrance to the chimney. The chimney is a class III climb. At the top of the chimney rests the 100-foot tree that fell into the wash. Scramble up the sandstone to the left of the tree. Both the wash and can-

Photo 7

yon divide ahead. Go into the right fork of the wash.

The trick from this point is to find the brush-free wash. The wash sits above and perpendicular to the one you're in, making it hard to locate. If you continue too far up the right fork of the wash, you'll start cussing the brush! Hike about 100 yards into the right fork of the wash and look for an opening in the brush on the left (west) side. Go through the opening, then immediately left into a dry creekbed. The creekbed intersects the brush-free

Photo 8

wash in about 30 yards. Go right (west) into the wash and continue bouldering.

In about 150 yards, you'll traverse the steep-slanted sandstone wall of the right (north) bank to the top of a cascading waterfall. Use the cracks and small ridges to help with the traverse. Photo 9 shows the start of the traverse. The top of the waterfall presents a great place to take a break.

After your break, go around the ponderosa pine and jump over the water. In about 75 yards you come to a spot where the water flows through a narrow channel. Stay to the right of the water, avoiding the slanted left wall. A path starts at the end of the water and stays to the right (north) of the water.

Photo 9

Photo 10

Photo 10 shows the boulder you have to straddle to climb over. Do not try to traverse the right wall. Once past the boulder, scramble up the waterfall on the right side.

Follow the wash to the next waterfall. Climb up on the left past the pinion pine. The water decreases as you make your way toward the backside of Mt. Wilson. When you cross another pool with a tree growing in the water, look for an opening in the brush on the left, which goes to the left (south) wall of the canyon. The route heads west, traveling along that south wall. Stay near it as a boulder field jets off to the right (north). Scramble up the dry waterfall that has a large boulder of gray limestone at the top. Photo 11 shows the section to climb; it lies above the waterfall you just climbed. This class III climb might be difficult for people with a limited reach. At the top of the climb are huge ponderosa pines over 100 feet tall. If the climb in Photo 11 is too tough, look for a faint path that starts at the far right of the dry waterfall.

At this point you can see the backside of Mt. Wilson tapering off. It eventually meets up with the wash. Find the path that lies about

Photo 11

30 feet from the south wall and follow it up the wash. The path goes to the right side of another huge limestone boulder. By this time you will have noticed that the wash appears more like a creekbed. You're getting close to the fault line that separates the sandstone from the limestone. Climb up the huge white boulders that divide the creekbed into left and right forks. Continue on the path as it leads to a 15-foot limestone boulder. Climb this boulder (class III) and continue fol-

Photo 12

lowing the path. The path drops into the creekbed, which empties to the right of a juniper. (See Photo 12.) Go between the

Photo 13

juniper and the boulder. Pick up the path as it heads SW. When the canyon divides, go onto the right fork. Follow the path as it heads due west along the right side of the creekbed. The path splits; take the lower one as it descends into the creekbed. The creekbed turns back into a wash. Hiking in the wash is faster than staying on the upper path. When a huge overhanging limestone boulder blocks the way, follow the path that travels to the right of the boulder. (See Photo 13.)

The path leads to a

Photo 14

couple of archways created by falling boulders. The archway to the right (not shown in Photo 14) is an easier climb. Past the archway, the path descends to the creekbed. Cross the creekbed (the wash has changed back to a creekbed) and scramble up the slabs above the small waterfall. Drop back into the creekbed and follow the path to the base of a huge ponderosa pine. About 30 yards past the pine, look for a path that leads out of the creekbed to the right. Once out of the creekbed it's a class I and II scramble to the peak. You should be at the peak in about an hour.

A cairn marks the start of the hard-to-follow scree path that heads NW (336 degrees) up the back of Mt. Wilson. Follow the path until you see the landscape change from red sandstone scree to gray limestone. This marks the fault line.

The idea is to stay near the fault line and head ENE (80 degrees) until you hike past the dry washes (this avoids hiking up and down the dry washes). Head for the dead tree that sits on the ridgeline. At the tree you'll see a false peak off to the NE (right); don't go that way. (See Photo 15.) A huge gorge

Sandstone Mountain

False Peak

Photo 15

lies before the white sandstone mountain in Photo 15. When you see a gully full of manzanita, walk to the top of it. You'll be at the base of the sandstone mountain in Photo 15. Climb up the sandstone mountain heading NNE (30 degrees). (See Photo 16).

Go here first

then toward this peak

Photo 16

The peak is not visible at the top of this mountain, but head toward the peak highlighted in Photo 16. Mt. Wilson peak lies behind the false peak in Photo 16 and is the only red-tipped peak. (See Photo 17.)

Mt. Wilson Peak

Photo 17

It's a class II climb to the peak. A sign-in book sits at the bottom of the cairn. As you can see by the few entries, you're at a place few people have ever been. Money, titles, or lies can't help someone climb this mountain. It takes hard work and determination. Relax, take in the view, and savor the moment. Be sure to eat; you'll need energy for the hike back to the trailhead.

To Descend: Retrace your steps. You'll find descending is much faster because you're able to climb down obstacles that you couldn't climb up. To be safe, you should have four or more hours of daylight left.

♦ ♦ ♦

Indecision Peak

Hike: Indecision Peak — up and back
Trailhead: First Creek pulloff — marked
Distance: 10 miles — round trip
Elevation gain: 2,010 feet
Elevation peak: 5,560 feet
Time: 9 hours
Difficulty: 5
Danger level: 5
How easy to follow: 5
Children: no
Map: Blue Diamond, NEV

Directions: Drive west on Charleston past Red Rock Canyon. Stay on Route 159 for five miles past the turnoff to Red Rock Canyon. Park at the signed First Creek parking area on the right (west) side of the road.

Overview: The **route** follows First Creek Trail for about a mile, then it's an assault straight up to the southernmost sandstone crag on the ridgeline. From there, it's a series of chutes and passages to the south-facing gully that leads to the peak.

Comments: This is a great hike with fantastic overlooks on the way up. Indecision Peak looks down on Bonnie Springs and Spring Mountain Ranch. Due to the length of the hike, it's best made during the longer spring days, but do not attempt this hike in hot weather. The sun scorches the hike's east-face approach. Mid-spring is the best time to enjoy the hike. Because of the brush, wear long pants and a sweatshirt.

"Shale" Rock

Boulder Field

Upper Bluffs

Photo 1

The Hike: Follow First Creek Trail, taking the left fork and going past the unmarked turnoff to the waterfall. Continue on the trail for a few hundred yards, then hike south (190 degrees) through the desert toward the base of Indecision. As you get closer, you'll see a lower and upper band of red sandstone bluffs. (See Photo 1.) Hike toward the base of the upper bluffs. The incline is strenuous. Once you reach the base, traverse south across the red dirt until reaching an east-facing gully. There is a faint path to follow. About 100 yards up, the gully turns into a boulder field as seen in Photo 1. Climb SSW (210 degrees) up the gully and into the boulder field. Although paths have been created on the sides of the boulder field, they are extremely steep, making climbing on the boulders a better option. The right (north) side of the boulder field is the preferred route. The boulder field is a strenuous class II climb. Be careful of dislodging boulders.

Once through the boulder field, the incline becomes moderate as you make your way to the left (south) side of the southernmost crag. This sandstone crag has a smooth sculptured face that makes it look like shale rock. (See Photo 2.) Climb over the boulders that lie in front of the "shale" rock. Make your way through the brushy chute seen in Photo 3. At the top of the chute, you'll be at the left-most edge of the shale-like rock. From here you want to go around the

Photo 2

backside (west side) of the rock and up into the correct gully that leads to the peak. Hike to the south side (250 degrees) of the "shale" rock to a chute blocked by manzanita bushes.

Photo 3

Scramble up the brownish-black-faced sandstone to the right of the bushes. Once above the bushes, go into the chute as shown in Photo 4. From this point look for cairns that help mark the way. Once at the top of this chute, head NW (330 degrees) alongside the sandstone ledges and into the alleyway as seen in Photo 5. Once in the alleyway, head toward the crag in Photo 5. If you're in the correct alleyway, you'll climb past a couple of dead trees. At the top of the alleyway, there's

Photo 4

a great overlook to the right. This may be the stopping point for those who find that this hike is a little too strenuous. If others in your party continue to the peak, you'll have a very long wait for them to return to this point. If you think this may apply to you, bring a book and read it at the overlook. You should not descend alone.

Once back from the overlook, go left (west) and climb up

Photo 5

Photo 6

the wall of sandstone. (See Photo 6.) Hike west along the base of the mound to a passage. At the passage you have two options: climb down the sandstone on the right side (class III) or go under the boulder. Continue along the base of the north wall. (See Photo 7.) Sandstone Canyon lies about 1,000 feet below to your left (south). About 100 yards ahead is the start of a huge gully that leads to the peak. Walk down the rock chips into the gully.

Photo 7

The brush in the first part of the gully is easily negotiated by staying near the right (east) wall of the gully. When it becomes too brushy along the wall, find the drainage that's hidden in the middle of the gully. This drainage weaves between the scrub oak and manzanita. Looking up the gully, you see sandstone crags dividing it into left and right courses. Head toward the large ponderosa pine that stands at the beginning of the right divide. (See Photo 8.) This class II climb up the right side goes up a wash to a second ponderosa pine. A huge gorge lies to the right; the drop-off is several hundred feet. Avoid this gorge for now by going to the left and up the chute in Photo 9. Cairns mark the chute. At the top of the chute, stay to the right and aim for the sandstone tower. Follow the cairns that even-

Ponderosa Pine

Photo 8

tually lead to a 15-foot-wide ledge that overlooks the gorge. The ledge empties into the gorge via a class I ramp. At this point, the gorge becomes a gully and it's only about 200 yards to the top. The first 100 yards involves avoiding brushy areas and, depending on your choices, some limited class III climbing. There's a tricky climb up when you first enter the gully.

Photo 9

Photo 10

You are still heading NE (310 degrees). The last 100 yards is easier.

At the top of this gully is a large flat area (perfect for camping, if only you could lug the gear to this point). Off to the right (NE) is a false peak. The real peak lies behind this peak and is the northernmost sandstone peak. Photo 10 shows the false peak. Walk about 100 yards NE around the west side of the false peak to the backside of the real peak. Look for the pine tree that lies between the two peaks. It's a short climb up the sandstone to the cairn that marks the peak. There's a sign-in book inside a coffee can. The peak offers great views of Las Vegas and, to the south, the southern peaks of Red Rock.

The real adventurous, who are in excellent shape, can go west past the limestone peak, NW around the end of First Creek, and NE up to Mt. Wilson. Follow the directions for the Mt. Wilson hike after leaving First Creek. The descent could be done through First Creek, making a closed loop out of one very long hike.

To Descend: Go down the gully and look for the ledge on the right side. Go up the ledge and down into the main gully. Stay to the right of the sandstone pinnacle while descending. When you come out of the chute in Photo 9, look for the ponderosa pine that marks the start of the wash. Climb down the wash to the next ponderosa pine. From this point, you can see the rock chips you walked across. Hike up the rock chips, go around to the north wall, and climb through the hole. Climb down the mound of sandstone and into the long alleyway that leads down to the backside of the "shale" rock. It is a SE descent (130 degrees). Once near the "shale," climb down and around to the front of it. Bear east, down to the boulder field. At the bottom of the boulder field, look for a dead tree on the left side that marks the traverse along the red sandstone bluffs. From here you can see the desert floor and First Creek Trail.

♦ ♦ ♦

Grand Circle

Hike: Grand Circle — closed loop
Trailhead: Moenkopi trailhead — marked
Distance: 11.3 miles
Elevation gain: 300 feet
Elevation peak: no peak
Time: 5 hours
Difficulty: 3
Danger level: 1
How easy to follow: 2
Children: yes
Map: La Madre Mtn., Nev

Directions: Park at the Visitors Center. About 30 yards SW of the Visitors Center is the pavilion. The signed Moenkopi trailhead starts just west of the pavilion.

Overview: The **trail** passes next to Calico Hills, Sandstone Quarry, and White Rock Hills before heading back to the Visitors Center.

Comments: Hiking the Grand Circle gives you an appreciation of the enormity of Red Rock. The Grand Circle is part of many different trails. It has little elevation gain, allowing anyone who has the time to enjoy it.

The Hike: The trail starts off level as it heads in a westerly direction. It soon divides; take the right fork and continue as the trail crosses the Scenic Loop. It heads toward the Calico Hills area, which is a combination of red and white sandstone hills. When the trail deadends into an old gravel road, go left onto the gravel road as it parallels Calico Hills. Near the one-mile point, the trail reaches Calico Hills Overlook I parking lot and appears to end. Hike down the Calico Hills Overlook I trail, which heads straight (NE) into Calico Hills. Caution is urged; the trail descends rapidly on loose gravel. Go left at the first fork. If you hike onto the sandstone, you've gone too far.

The trail heads west and parallels Calico Hills. It never goes up into the sandstone crags of Calico Hills. As the trail descends, it goes across numerous sandstone slabs, only to continue on the far side of each interruption of sandstone. The trail begins to climb as it heads toward Calico II Overlook. This is a favorite area for rock climbers. Photo 1 shows the trail as it descends to the left, down the red sandstone. At the bot-

Photo 1

tom, the trail resumes across more red sandstone for about 20 yards. When the trail seems to stop, go left, stepping up onto a red sandstone slab. From this point, scramble down the narrow chute. At the bottom of this chute, look for the gray rocks that mark the left boundary of the dirt trail. (See Photo 2.) The trail crosses over several slabs of sandstone as it follows the wash. Look for four or five large gray rocks at the end of a long stretch of sandstone. Go to the left of the gray rocks and follow the dirt trail once again. (See Photo 3.) When the trail comes to a three-

Photo 2

Photo 3

way divide, take the left fork. As the trail heads toward the Calico Hills II Overlook parking lot, hike past the first fork on the right, but turn onto the second fork. If you end up at the Calico Hills II Overlook parking lot, you missed the turnoff.

The trail crosses over a large slab of red sandstone and resumes on the other side. Stay on the main trail; do not take any of the numerous forks. At the two-mile mark, you pass the petroglyph rock. (See Photo 4.)

The incline is moderate as the trail heads westerly. The trail intersects the Sandstone Quarry parking lot at the SE corner. Go to the far end (west) of the parking lot and onto the signed trail for Turtlehead Peak and Calico Tanks. About 75 yards into this segment of the trail, it empties into a large wash. Go left across

Photo 4

the wash and look for a small sign that marks the continuation of the Grand Circle Trail. Gray rocks outline this part of the trail. If you go past the refrigerator-sized sandstone blocks, you've gone too far. The trail crosses another wash as it heads SW toward a minor hill.

At about four miles, the trail crosses the Scenic Loop road and heads SW. When the trail drops down into another wash, look for the juniper that marks the continuation of the trail. The Scenic Loop is crossed again at about the five-mile point.

The paved and then gravel road that intersects the Scenic Loop becomes part of the Grand Circle Trail. Follow it to the upper parking lot of the White Rock Springs area. In the left corner of the circular parking lot is the trailhead for the White Rock/Willow Springs/La Madre Trail. Follow this trail for about 100 yards and go left at the fork onto the abandoned gravel road. This part of the trail has a slight decline as it passes to the east of White Rock Hills. The trail drops into a ravine. At the bottom of the ravine, the trail goes to the left and weaves through a patch of bushes before climbing out of the ravine. After the trail climbs out of the ravine, it travels down into a depression, which is a collecting place for water, evident by the amount of trees and vegetation.

A small ridge to the east is the next designation. Once over the ridge, start looking for the continuation of the Grand Circle Trail that intersects from the SE (left side). Remember, you are currently on the White Rock/Willow Springs/La Madre Trail. If you see the turnoff road for Willow Springs, you've gone too far. It's a paved road that turns off the Scenic Loop and heads west (right).

Go left onto the unmarked Grand Circle Trail. The trail crosses the Scenic Loop in about a quarter of a mile. About 300 yards after crossing the Scenic Loop, the trail deteriorates into an abandoned jeep trail and heads SE toward the Visitors Center which is about three and a half miles away. You'll pass boulders that look out of place as you hike SE on the level trail. The white arrows in Photo 5 show the direction of travel .

Photo 5

At about nine miles, you pass a large cairn, and you might see the sun's reflection off car windows parked at the Visitors

Center. The trail heads left into a wash that it has been following. Cross the wash and pick up the jeep trail on the far side of the wash. At this point, a ridge blocks your view of the Visitors Center, but continue to travel toward it. The trail crosses another wash and becomes easier to follow. It soon intersects the Moenkopi Trail. Turn right at this intersection and head toward the Visitors Center. The Grand Circle ends where it began.

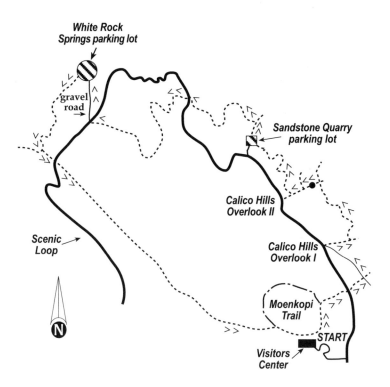

◆ ◆ ◆

Moenkopi Loop

Hike: Moenkopi Loop — closed loop
Trailhead: Moenkopi Loop — marked
Distance: 2 miles
Elevation gain: 100 feet
Elevation peak: no peak
Time: 1 hour
Difficulty: 1
Danger level: 1
How easy to follow: 1
Children: yes
Map: La Madre Mtn., NEV

Directions: Park at the Visitors Center. About 30 yards SW of the Visitors Center is a pavilion. The signed Moenkopi trailhead starts just west of the pavilion.

Overview: The **trail** heads west, gains a ridgeline, and drops into a wash before returning.

Comments: A great walking trail for beginners or for visitors who want to do more than just drive the Scenic Loop.

The Hike: The trail starts off level as it heads west. When it forks, go left and admire the view of Calico Hills. The other fork travels to Calico Hills I Overlook. As the trail's grade increases, Turtlehead Peak rises above the sandstone in Calico Hills. The trail passes yucca, creosote bushes, and scrub oak as it makes its way to a ridgeline in the direction of Mt. Wilson.

The trail climbs a small hill and stays on the crest of the ridgeline as it continues in a southerly direction. Grayish rocks, part of an ancient seabed millions of years ago, are embedded in the trail.

A second fork comes in on the right side of the trail. You can take either trail, since they meet in about 300 yards. If you go right at this fork, the trail descends as it heads in the direction of Mt. Wilson and Rainbow Peak. It soon deadends into the original Moenkopi Trail. Go right at this intersection and follow the trail as it descends SE. The main trail stays on the ridgeline, then descends the backside and meets at the fork. Stay on the main trail; going right sends you in the wrong direction.

The trail drops into a wash and heads due east toward the Visitors Center. As you climb a hill, the Grand Circle Trail comes in at a sharp angle from the right. The trail makes its way back to the Visitors Center and ends where it began.

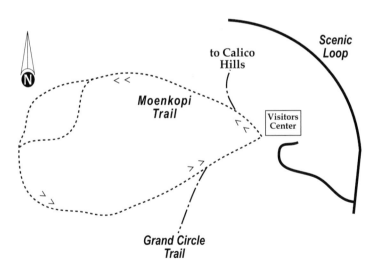

♦ ♦ ♦

Cave Canyon

Hike: Cave Canyon — up and back
Trailhead: Horse Stables pull-off on 159 — marked
Distance: 3 miles — round trip
Elevation gain: 350 feet
Elevation peak: no peak
Time: 2 hours
Difficulty: 2
Danger level: 1
How easy to follow: 1
Children: yes
Map: Blue Diamond, NEV

Directions: The trailhead is located at the gravel parking lot on the east (left) side on State Route 159, about a mile past the turnoff to Red Rock Canyon.

Overview: The **trail** weaves through a canyon, ending at a small cave.

Comments: A good hike for beginners and for people who like caves.

The Hike: Weave around the gate that bars vehicle access to the dirt road. (See Photo 1.) In about ten yards, turn right at the trail sign. The trail heads east with no elevation gain as it travels toward the horse stables. The burnt landscape near the stables serve as a reminder of how vulnerable the desert is to fire. The trail crosses the same dirt road and continues on the other side. Once past the stables, you head south into a canyon. (See Photo 2.) The incline increases as the trail climbs to the top of a small hill. At the junction, go left and continue hiking into the canyon. A section of wooden steps eases the ascent as the trail climbs to the west wall of the canyon. The trail forks, then reunites 50 yards ahead. The canyon walls rise up more than 100 feet. The trail ascends another incline before terminating at a small cave along the west wall.

You can explore further by dropping into the wash and climbing up the dry waterfall using the pile of rocks. It's a class III climb up the waterfall and even trickier climbing back down.

To Descend: Retrace your steps.

Photo 1

Photo 2

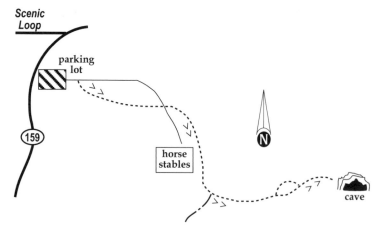

♦ ♦ ♦

Fossil Canyon

Hike: Fossil Canyon — up and back or closed loop
Trailhead: Horse Stables pull-off on 159 — marked
Distance: 4 miles or 6 miles — round trip
Elevation gain: 400 or 700 feet
Elevation peak: no peak
Time: 2 or 3 hours
Difficulty: 3
Danger level: 2
How easy to follow: 2
Children: yes
Map: La Madre Mtn., NEV and Blue Diamond, NEV

Directions: The trailhead is located at the gravel parking lot on the east (left) side on State Route 159, about a mile past the turn off to Red Rock Canyon.

Overview: The **trail** leads to the mouth of the canyon, then it's a **route** through the canyon.

Comments: This hike offers a couple of options. You can hike up and back through the canyon or connect with the Fossil Ridge Trail, making a closed loop out of the hike. You can make the hike longer by hiking into a side canyon.

The Hike: Weave around the gate that bars vehicle access to the dirt road. (See Photo 1.) In about ten yards, turn right at the trail sign. The trail heads east with no elevation gain as it travels toward the horse stables. The burnt landscape near the stables serves as a reminder of how vulnerable the desert is to fire. The trail crosses the same dirt road and continues on the other side. Once past the stables, the trail heads SE toward a large canyon. (See Photo 2.) The trail climbs to the top of a small hill where it merges with another trail. About 40 yards past this fork, go right onto a path that comes in from the south. The path immediately crosses

Photo 1

a wash as it heads SSE (150 degrees) into a different canyon. You'll stay on the east side of the canyon for about a quarter mile before descending, then you'll ascend the west side of the canyon. Ancient seabed rock that contains fossils lines the wash. The walls of the canyon are still steep, rising about 75 feet to the ridge. The path empties into the wash and the hike becomes a class II bouldering route.

Heading SE through the wash, you'll come upon a huge boulder that has fallen into the wash and formed a shelter that resembles a cave entrance. The walls of the canyon decrease in height and steepness after passing the boulder and the hike becomes a class I route again. When the canyon bends to the left (east), look up toward the right (west) and you'll see large brownish boulders sitting at the top of the ridgeline. These are the same boulders you pass

Photo 2

Photo 3

on the Fossil Ridge hike.

At this point you've hiked about two miles and have a number of options: you can continue up the wash for another mile and a half, connect with the Fossil Ridge Trail that returns to the trailhead, or turn around and retrace your steps back to the trailhead. If you want to hike up to Fossil Ridge now or after continuing up the wash, look for the brownish boulder in Photo 3 and climb up the west wall as outlined in the photo. If you pass a brownish boulder about the size of a car, you've gone about 20 yards too far in the wash. Once you climb out of the wash, head toward the boulders until you come to the path. Go right (north) on the path and make another right when the path divides. You'll be heading NW. The path follows the ridge and overlooks the canyon you just hiked through. For a complete description, see the Fossil Ridge hike (p. 263). It's about two miles back to the trailhead.

If you continue in the wash, the pace is easy as you hike over the ancient bedrock. About 200 yards past the turnoff for the Fossil Ridge path, the wash divides. Go into the left (east) wash by climbing onto its north bank to avoid the brush. You can drop back down into the wash in about 75 yards. You'll be heading ENE (75 degrees) as you boulder your way up the class II wash. The incline becomes strenuous in parts. The canyon walls become less steep as the incline decreases. When the wash becomes brushy, hike up on the north bank and parallel it. At this point the canyon walls have disappeared and the wash becomes a drainage. You hike past a variety of cacti and other desert plants. Soon a 100-foot pile of dirt comes into view. The dirt is on private property and indicates the turning-around point.

To Descend: Retrace your steps. Go right (north) into the original wash. If you want to return on the Fossil Ridge path, look for the boulders on the left (west) ridge. (See Photo 4.) From this side you can walk up to the boulders, since the canyon walls have not formed. Once near the boulders, head NW alongside them until you come to the path. Returning by Fossil Ridge path is a little longer, but quicker.

Photo 4

♦ ♦ ♦

Visitors Center Overlook

Hike: Visitors Center Overlook — up and back or closed loop
Trailhead: Horse Stables pulloff on 159 — marked
Distance: 1.5 miles — round trip
Elevation gain: 250 feet
Elevation peak: no peak
Time: 1 hour
Difficulty: 1
Danger level: 1
How easy to follow: 1
Children: yes
Map: Blue Diamond, NEV.

Directions: The trailhead is located at the gravel parking lot on the east (left) side on State Route 159, about a mile past the turnoff to Red Rock Canyon.

Overview: The **trail** climbs a hill and goes to an overlook.

Comments: A quick and easy hike that rewards the hiker with a great view of Red Rock Canyon. The hike can be done as a closed loop.

The Hike: Weave around the gate that bars vehicle access to the dirt road. (See Photo 1.) Follow it for about 150 yards. Take the first fork that comes in on the left. Follow the fork for about 30 yards until it intersects a trail. Make a right onto the trail as it heads NE. When the trail divides, go left and follow it up a foothill. The incline becomes moderate as it ascends switchbacks. Hoof prints indicate that this trail is shared with horseback riders.

The grade levels out at the top of the foothill as the trail heads NNE. Look for fossils in the ancient seabed rock along the trail. The grade becomes moderate again as the trail heads NNE and climbs a second foothill. Another trail comes in

Photo 1

from the left (west); take it on the way back if you want to make a loop out of the hike. The trail ends when it comes to a high point and makes a circle. The overlook offers a good view of Red Rock, the Visitors Center, and State Route 159.

To Descend: Retrace your steps or go right (west) onto the trail mentioned above. The alternative trail makes an easy descent off the foothill toward State Route 159. It then parallels State Route 159 back to the parking lot. If it has rained recently, don't descend by this trail—it will be too muddy.

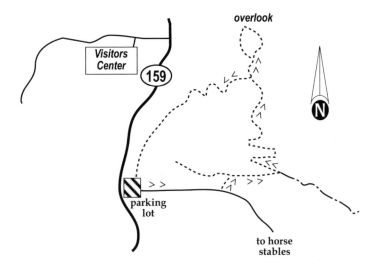

♦ ♦ ♦

Fossil Ridge

Hike: Fossil Ridge — closed loop
Trailhead: Horse Stables pulloff on 159 — marked
Distance: 3 miles
Elevation gain: 400 feet
Elevation peak: no peak
Time: 2 hours
Difficulty: 2
Danger level: 1
How easy to follow: 2
Children: yes
Map: La Madre Mtn., NEV and Blue Diamond, NEV

Directions: The trailhead is located at the gravel parking lot
on the east (left) side on State Route 159, about a mile past the
turnoff to Red Rock Canyon.

Overview: The **path** makes a large circle to the south and follows a ridge that overlooks a canyon as it makes its way back
to the parking lot.

Comments: The hike offers a chance to see fossils that are
millions of years old, and a good overlook into a canyon.

The Hike: Weave around the gate that bars vehicle access to
the dirt road. (See Photo 1.) Immediately turn right onto the
first of three trails/paths that head SSE. The path is not marked.
The incline is flat as you pass scrub oak and a variety of cacti.
In about a mile, the path climbs a minor ridge and passes large
concrete-looking boulders. Once on the ridge, the path flattens out and travels east. The incline becomes moderate as the

path climbs a foothill. Turn around and look to the west to get a great view of Bridge Mountain, Rainbow Peak, Oak Creek, and Pine Creek.

Photo 1

The path continues SSE as it passes a few highway-type signs that have been faded by the sun. Soon after the path turns and heads in a NE direction, a large pile of brown boulders appears. (See Photo 2.) The path weaves behind the boulders and soon divides. Take the left fork heading NW that follows the ridgeline of Blue Diamond Hill as it parallels the canyon to the east. The canyon floor, about 75 feet below, is part of the Fossil Canyon hike. Along this section of the path, fossils are found in the ancient sea bedrock. The hike comes to an overlook that offers a good view of the canyon below. The path disappears as it crosses a large dirt area; look NW and you'll spot the continuation of the path. As the path starts to descend the ridgeline, the parking lot comes into view. The horse stables lie below and to the east of the ridgeline.

At the fork, a major path comes in from the right, which weaves down the hill to the horse stables. From here you can follow the dirt road back to the parking lot, or if you want to stay up on the ridge, continue NW on the original path. When the path fades, go to the right (east) and try to pick it up. If you

can't find it, continue NW until you see it descending off the ridge and heading toward the parking lot, which is now less than 300 yards away. The path ends a few feet from where it began by the gate.

Photo 2

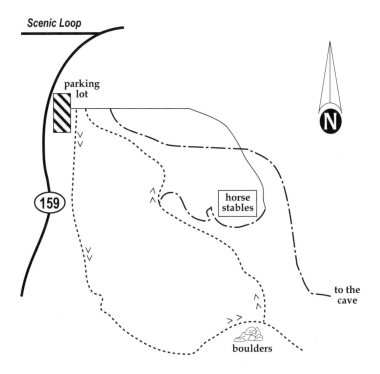

◆ ◆ ◆

Las Vegas Overlook

Hike: Las Vegas Overlook — up and back
Trailhead: Horse Stables pulloff on 159 — marked
Distance: 4 miles — round trip
Elevation gain: 540 feet
Elevation peak: 4,400 feet
Time: 3 hours
Difficulty: 3
Danger level: 2
How easy to follow : 2
Children: yes
Map: Blue Diamond, NEV

Directions: The trailhead is located at the large parking lot on the east (left) side on State Route 159, about a mile past the turnoff to Red Rock Canyon.

Overview: The **route** follows a wash up a gully to the overlook.

Comments: A spectacular overlook of Las Vegas is waiting for you at the top. Although this is a route, it's easy to follow.

The Hike: Weave around the gate that bars vehicle access to the dirt road. (See Photo 1.) Continue on the dirt road for about 150 yards where two forks intersect the road as it bends to the right. Take the second fork, heading NE toward the muffin-looking boulders on the ridgeline. (Photo 2 shows the boulders and an overview of the hike.) The fork goes across one wash and empties into a second one. A horse trail crosses the wash; remain in the wash and continue toward the gully that

leads up to the muf-
fin-looking boulder.
It's easy walking in
the wash. When the
wash divides, take
the right fork and
continue NE toward
the ridgeline. The
washes come to-
gether about 200
yards in front of the
base of the mountain

Photo 1

that the muffin boulders rest on.

At the base of the mountain, a minor wash comes in from
the right (south). Go into this wash and follow it as it leads
into the gully that goes to the muffin boulders. At times, it
might be easier to climb out of the wash on the left (east) side
to avoid the boulders. As you go into the gully, the incline
becomes moderate. The floor of the wash is ancient seabed
rock, containing million-year-old fossils.

You can avoid most of the climbing (mainly class II) by
hiking out of the wash on the left (north) side. When you come
to the 20-foot-high cliff wall, go left of the wall and follow the
path to the top of the cliff. You'll encounter a second cliff wall
about 40 feet high. A chute along the extreme left side of the
wall provides an
easy way up. Use the
wall to aid in your
climb up the chute.
(See Photo 3.)

Muffin Boulders

Photo 2

From the top of
the wall you've just
climbed around,
you'll see a third cliff.
The right (south) end
of the cliff provides
the best way up and
over. That was the
last cliff wall. From

here the route be-
comes easier. Once
the gully starts to flat-
ten out, look for the
muffin boulders,
which will be to the
north (left) of the
wash. (See Photo 4.)

Head up the hill
to the boulders. From
there travel SE (110
degrees) for about 75
yards to the edge of

Photo 3

the ridgeline. Look east for a panoramic view of the casinos, the congestion, and the smog of Las Vegas. You'll be thankful you're here, in this peaceful and scenic place, and not down there.

To Descend: Retrace your steps.

Photo 4

♦GLOSSARY♦

bouldering—Using hands and feet to climb over, around, or down large boulders. Most bouldering routes are in the canyons of Red Rock.

bristlecone pine—A twisted knotty pine, less than 60 feet tall, found above 9,000 feet. They have short needles in bunches of five. They live to be thousands of years old.

buttress—A large flat portion of rock that stands out from a wall behind it.

cairn—A pile of rocks used to mark a path or route.

canyon—A deep narrow valley with high steep sides.

chute—A steep well-worn passage where debris often funnels down from a mountain. It is larger than a crack and smaller than a gully.

closed loop trail/path—A trail or path that makes a complete circle.

chimney—A steep narrow chute with parallel walls.

crack—A parallel-sided fracture in a rock, varying in size from a hair to several feet.

crag—A sandstone wall scaled by technical climbers.

declination—The angle that a freely turning magnetic needle makes with the imaginary line that points to true north.

face—The steep side of a mountain, normally more than 40 degrees.

gully—A broad, normally low-angled, depression that runs vertically down the side of a mountain.

juniper—15-30 feet tall with scale-like leaves in clusters of three. They produce gray berries.

open loop trail/path—A trail or path that makes an incomplete circle. The trailhead and ending destination are in different locations. Two cars may be required; one parked at the trailhead, the other at the final destination.

pass—Obvious cleft or break in a ridgeline where it is possible to cross.

path—A non-maintained pathway. It's harder to follow than a trail, but easier to follow than a route. Some paths were once trails that, because of little usage, have become overgrown or faded.

pinion pine—A short pine with short single needles on the twigs.

ponderosa pine—A tall pine, which can grow up to 100 feet tall, with long needles in clusters of three.

ramp—An inclined sandstone ledge.

ravine—A small, narrow, steep-sided valley larger than a gully and smaller than a canyon.

rock scrambling—Climbing up and over rock without the use of ropes. Class II- and III-type climbing. Most prominent in the Red Rock area.

route—A trek that's hiked by landmarks. There are no trails or paths to follow.

sandstone—Porous rock made of sand. Found at Red Rock.

scree—An accumulation of small rocks, typically at the bottom of a slope.

scrub oak—Spiny, many-branched, thicket-forming scrub; occasionaly a small tree. The leaves are irregularly shaped, with sharp pointy ends that tear clothing and skin.

slope—A very low-angled face of a mountain.

summit—The peak of a mountain.

suzan—A line of small rocks that marks the way. They are used as landmarks when the terrain is too steep to make a cairn.

switchback—The zigzags in a trail or path that make it easier to go up the side of a mountain.

talus—Loose rock and gravel that lie on a slope.

topo map—A map showing the details of the contour of the land by means of lines and symbols.

trail—A well-maintained pathway that is easy to follow.

trailhead—The starting point of a trail, path, or route.

yucca—A small shrub, usually with clustered trunks and green bayonet-like leaves, which can grow up to 15 feet tall and has white or purplish flowers.

About the Author

Branch Whitney first visited the mountains (Rockies) at the tender age of seven and knew immediately that he wanted to climb them. Within two weeks of moving to Las Vegas in 1983, he bagged Mt. Charleston. Since then, he's logged more than 1,000 miles hiking the trails, paths, and routes surrounding Las Vegas. These days, he stays busy as a hike leader for the Sierra Club and the Las Vegas Mountaineer's Club.

The companion Web site for *Hiking Las Vegas* can be found at www.hikinglasvegas.com. The Web site features more than 500 pages of hiking information, updates to this book, safety tips, color photos, enhanced topo maps, and additional hikes from around the Southwest.

About Huntington Press

Huntington Press is a specialty publisher of gambling- and Las Vegas-related books and periodicals, including the award winning consumer newsletter, *Anthony Curtis' Las Vegas Advisor*. To receive a copy of the Huntington Press catalog, call **1-800-244-2224** or write to the address below.

Huntington Press
3687 South Procyon Avenue
Las Vegas, Nevada 89103

Hiking
Southern Nevada
50 New Hikes

213 Pages • $17.95us

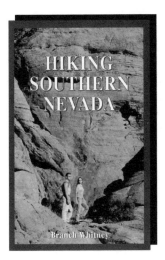

The author of the best-selling *Hiking Las Vegas* details 50 new adventures-on-foot within an hour's drive of the bright lights of Las Vegas. Step-by-step directions, easy-to-follow maps, and quick-reference features guide you along the best trails in the area. From the multicolored sandstone of Red Rock Canyon and Valley of Fire to the crisp air and serenity of Mt. Charleston and the hot springs of Lake Mead, *Hiking Southern Nevada* is indispensable for anyone who wants to experience this magnificent corner of the Southwest.

To order call:
1-800-244-2224

And now a message from our author, Branch Whitney.

I've recently been logging some heavy miles on the trails gathering information for my new book *Hiking Southern Nevada*. It features additional hikes in Red Rock Canyon and Mt. Charleston, and covers new ground in Valley of Fire State Park and Lake Mead National Recreation Area.

I'm interested in hearing from my fellow hiking enthusiasts. Anyone who would like to share ideas, tips, favorite hikes, or noteworthy experiences on the trails of southern Nevada can send them to me at the address below.

Branch Whitney
c/o Huntington Press
3687 South Procyon Avenue
Las Vegas, Nevada 89103
e-mail: books@huntingtonpress.com